NEW TESTAMENT
EVERYDAY BIBLE STUDY SERIES

NEW TESTAMENT
EVERYDAY BIBLE STUDY SERIES

1 & 2 TIMOTHY, TITUS, AND PHILEMON

WISDOM FOR EVERY CHURCH LEADER

SCOT MCKNIGHT

QUESTIONS WRITTEN BY
BECKY CASTLE MILLER

 Harper*Christian*
Resources

*New Testament Everyday Bible Study Series: 1 & 2 Timothy, Titus,
and Philemon*
© 2023 by Scot McKnight

Requests for information should be addressed to:
HarperChristian Resources, 3900 Sparks Dr. SE, Grand Rapids, Michigan
49546

ISBN 978-0-310-12951-6 (softcover)
ISBN 978-0-310-12952-3 (ebook)

First Printing May 2023 / Printed in the United States of America
23 24 25 26 27 LBC 5 4 3 2 1

For Laura Mott Tarro,
pastor

CONTENTS

1 TIMOTHY

2 TIMOTHY

TITUS

PHILEMON

GENERAL
INTRODUCTION

Christians make a claim for the Bible not made of any other book. Or, since the Bible is a library shelf of many authors, it's a claim we make of no other shelf of books. We claim that God worked in each of the authors as they were writing so that what was scratched on papyrus expressed what God wanted communicated to the people of God. Which makes the New Testament (NT) a book unlike any other book. Which is why Christians are reading the NT almost two thousand years later with great delight. These books have the power to instruct us and to rebuke us and to correct us and to train us to walk with God every day. We read these books because God speaks to us in them.

Developing a routine of reading the Bible with an open heart, a receptive mind, and a flexible will is the why of the *New Testament Everyday Bible Studies*. But not every day will be the same. Some days we pause and take it in, and other days we stop and repent and lament and open ourselves to God's restoring graces. No one word suffices for what the Bible does to us. In fact, the Bible's view of the Bible can be found by reading Psalm 119, the longest chapter in the Bible, with 176 verses! It is a meditation on eight terms for what the Bible is and what the Bible does to those who listen and read it. Its laws (*torah*) instruct us, its laws (*mishpat*) order us, its statutes direct us, its precepts inform us, its decrees guide us, its commands compel us, its words speak to us, and its promises comfort us. It is no wonder that the author can sum up all eight as the "way" (119:3). Each of those terms still speaks to what happens when we open our minds to the Word of God.

Every day with the Bible then is new because our timeless and timely God communes with us in our daily lives in our world and in our time. Just as God spoke to Jesus in Galilee and Paul in Ephesus and John on Patmos. These various contexts help us hear God in our context, so the *New Testament Everyday Bible Studies* will often delve into contexts. Most of us now have a Bible on our devices. We may well have several translations available to us everywhere we go every day. To hear those words, we are summoned by God to open the Bible, to attune our hearts to God, and to listen to what God says. My prayer is that these daily study guides will help each of us become daily Bible readers attentive to the mind of God.

INTRODUCTION: READING 1 & 2 TIMOTHY, TITUS, AND PHILEMON

The books of 1 and 2 Timothy, Titus, and Philemon are four letters to three pastoral leaders—Timothy, Titus, and Philemon. The letters do not explicitly instruct about leadership so much as they model a sage or two (Paul and Timothy wrote the letter to Philemon) advising and mentoring other leaders how to conduct themselves as leaders in the churches of Ephesus, Crete, and Colossae. This study guide keeps leaders of all sorts and at every level in mind as receivers of some sage's wisdom. When combined as they are in this study guide, these four letters become a collection of leadership wisdom—of course, tied to specific contexts with specific purposes. Again, these letters do not intend to reveal Paul's wisdom on leadership per se. But in Paul's mentoring of these three leaders, the letters do reveal important elements of leadership.

We name the first three letters in this study guide the "Pastoral Epistles" though the word "pastor" never appears in their pages. Yet no term is more appropriate. In the first two letters, Paul pastors Timothy about how to pastor the Ephesians, in the second he pastors Titus for the Cretans, and in the fourth letter, Paul pastors Philemon on how to pastor his house church. I'm a fan of the word "pastor" in a way I am not of the word "leader." Over the years I have griped about the abundant use of "leader" in church discussions, but I have chosen to use the term in this study guide for a reason. It gives me the opportunity to redefine the term "leader" with the activities of the pastor. These letters effectively remove the word "leader" from the business world and place it firmly in the middle of a church. Once there, the term "leader" morphs back into the word "pastor." It must be said, too, that I don't limit the word "pastor" to the guy who preaches on Sunday morning or the one who has a big office in the church building. I use it for anyone who pastors—that is, who mentors and cares for people and mentors them into the way of Jesus.

Even though these four letters come from unique situations, timeless wisdom pokes its way through every passage—from public affirmations of leaders to public criticisms of false teachers to "qualifications" of various positions in the church to how to conduct oneself in church services to women teaching and widow lists . . . and I could go on. There is much for every sort of church leader: parents, Sunday school teachers, small group ministers, pastors, preachers, and teachers. Business leaders too.

WORKS CITED IN THIS STUDY GUIDE

Fee, Gordon D. *1 and 2 Timothy, Titus*. New International Bible Commentary. Peabody, MA: Hendrickson, 1988. (Fee, *1 and 2 Timothy, Titus*)

Hoklotubbe, T. Christopher. *Civilized Piety: The Rhetoric of Pietas in the Pastoral Epistles and the*

Roman Empire. Waco, TX: Baylor University Press, 2017. (Hoklotubbe, *Civilized Piety*)

McKnight, Scot. *1 and 2 Timothy, and Titus*. New Cambridge Bible Commentary. New York: Cambridge University Press, 2023 forthcoming. (McKnight, *1 and 2 Timothy, and Titus*)

———. "*Eusebeia* as Social Respectability: The Public Life of the Christian Pastor." Pages 157–74 in *Rhetoric, History, and Theology: Interpreting the New Testament*. Edited by Todd D. Still and Jason A. Meyers. Lanham, MD: Lexington/Fortress Academic, 2021. (McKnight, "*Eusebeia*")

———. *The Letter to Philemon*. New International Commentary on the New Testament. Grand Rapids: Eerdmans, 2017. (McKnight, *Philemon*)

———. *The Second Testament: A New Translation*. Downers Grove, IL: IVP Academic, 2023. (McKnight, *The Second Testament*)

Towner, Philip H. *The Letters to Timothy and Titus*. New International Critical Commentary. Grand Rapids: Eerdmans, 2006. (Towner, *Letters*)

1 TIMOTHY

LEADERS KNOW THEIR CHRIST-RELATION

1 Timothy 1:1–2

¹ Paul, an apostle of Christ Jesus by the command of God our Savior and of Christ Jesus our hope,

² To Timothy my true son in the faith:

Grace, mercy and peace from God the Father and Christ Jesus our Lord.

Another letter, from about the same time Paul wrote this letter to his "true son in the faith" (1:2), begins as most letters we have discovered from the first century begin: "Heraklous to Pompeius greeting and continual good health." The sender (Heraklous) is followed by the addressee (Pompeius) with a greeting and wish for good health.

Paul's letters followed the custom of the day, but that custom was not left alone. Paul turned the common elements of a letter into a Christian kind of letter. His relationship to Timothy is a Christ-relation, and Timothy's relation to Paul is also a Christ-relation. They are united with each other only because Christ has united them.

In the heat of Hitler's pressures against the faithful in

the church of Germany, Dietrich Bonhoeffer reminded his students, who were hiding and on the run at times, that

> Christian community means community through Jesus Christ and in Jesus Christ. There is no Christian community that is more than this, and none that is less than this. . . . Christian community is solely this. We belong to one another only through and in Jesus Christ." (Bonhoeffer, *Life Together*, 31)

I speak for myself. I have a relationship to my bishop, Todd Hunter, because of a Christ-relation. I have a relationship to my pastors, Amanda Holm Rosengren and Stephanie Booth, because of a Christ-relation. I have a relation with my colleagues Lynn Cohick and Nijay Gupta because of a Christ-relation. Let's put it this way: I did not form the relations with them, nor did they form the relations with me. Christ formed the relationships. These are Christ-relations.

Notice what Paul does to the common greeting because of this Christ-relation. He defines himself as an "apostle of Christ Jesus" who was himself ordered by "God our Savior" and also by "Christ Jesus," who is "our hope" (1:1). Had he added "through the Spirit," we'd have had a full Trinitarian opening. The letter is to Timothy, which leads to a second Christ-relation of this letter's opening: Paul designates Timothy as "my true son in the faith" (1:2). The word "son" in the NIV could be better translated as "child," since the Greek term (*teknon*) commonly refers to a child, but the sense of child in this verse is that Paul is Timothy's spiritual parent—leading him to Christ and mentoring him in discipleship and, as well, in leadership (Galatians 4:19, 31; Romans 8:16–17, 21; 1 Corinthians 4:14; Philippians 2:15).

Paul's wish or blessings baptize the whole letter in terms that sound routine but develop major Christ-relation senses:

Grace is about God's love that forms a bond with those who receive his gifts and who then become agents of such grace to others. *Mercy* refers to God's love for those who suffer or who are sinful and outside God's grace, while *peace*, the common greeting of the ancient world at least echoes the powerful peace we have with God and with others because of Christ. To be sure, Timothy would have heard these words as both "hello" and "more than hello." They are "more than" because these three Christian virtues originate in "God the Father and Christ Jesus our Lord" (1:2). These virtues, too, are Christ-relations.

QUESTIONS FOR REFLECTION AND APPLICATION

1. What does it mean for Timothy to be Paul's spiritual child?

2. How does grace create bonds?

3. How does mercy showcase God's love in relationships?

4. How does peace impact our Christ-relations?

5. Who are some people you have Christ-relations with?

FOR FURTHER READING

Bonhoeffer, Dietrich. *Life Together, Prayerbook of the Bible*. Dietrich Bonhoeffer Works, volume 5. Edited by Geffrey B. Kelley. Translated by Daniel W. Bloesch and James H. Burtness. Minneapolis: Fortress, 2005.

LEADERS
LEAD WITH
THE GOSPEL

1 Timothy 1:3–11

³ *As I urged you when I went into Macedonia, stay there in Ephesus so that you may command certain people not to teach false doctrines any longer* ⁴ *or to devote themselves to myths and endless genealogies. Such things promote controversial speculations rather than advancing God's work—which is by faith.* ⁵ *The goal of this command is love, which comes from a pure heart and a good conscience and a sincere faith.* ⁶ *Some have departed from these and have turned to meaningless talk.* ⁷ *They want to be teachers of the law, but they do not know what they are talking about or what they so confidently affirm.*

⁸ *We know that the law is good if one uses it properly.* ⁹ *We also know that the law is made not for the righteous but for lawbreakers and rebels, the ungodly and sinful, the unholy and irreligious, for those who kill their fathers or mothers, for murderers,* ¹⁰ *for the sexually immoral, for those practicing homosexuality, for slave traders and liars and perjurers—and for whatever else is contrary to the sound doctrine* ¹¹ *that conforms to the gospel concerning the glory of the blessed God, which he entrusted to me.*

The one who knows most what love of another person is, is the one who immediately recognizes when love is in jeopardy. Those who know the system best are the ones who perceive when the system is compromised. Those who know the gospel best are the ones who recognize when someone saying something about the gospel is actually hopping lanes. I believe each of these lines, but I also know that not everyone has the capacity to perceive false teachings. I also know that the word "heresy" (or "heretic") needs to be used only by experts in theology and only after someone has been examined by those experts in theology. The word ought not to be stuck on people's heads by social media content creators.

Paul knows the gospel, he knows Timothy knows the same gospel, and Paul wants his "true son in the faith" to correct those who are corrupting the gospel.

LEADERS LEAD BY KNOWING THE GOSPEL

The standard for Christian belief is the gospel, but we have to wait until the end of today's passage for the standard to be stated: "and for whatever else is contrary to the sound doctrine that conforms to the gospel concerning the glory of the blessed God, which he entrusted to me" (1:10b–11). Sound doctrine is measured by the gospel, and the gospel is articulated with striking clarity in 1 Corinthians 15:3–5:

> What I received I passed on to you as of first importance: that Christ died for our sins according to the Scriptures, that he was buried, that he was raised on the third day according to the Scriptures, and that he appeared to Cephas, and then to the Twelve.

One could argue that Paul's gospel standard also includes the appearances of 1 Corinthians 15:6–8, or one could argue that the gospel includes everything God does between the birth and second coming of Christ (15:3–28). Yes to each of those, but it does seem Paul's crisp formula at 15:3–5 articulates the gospel. One can add to this the even more crisp 2 Timothy 2:8 ("Remember Jesus Christ, raised from the dead, descended from David. This is my gospel."), or turn to Romans 10:9–10, where the gospel is a raised "Jesus is Lord." What matters is that leaders know the gospel and know that the gospel is the standard for the orthodox faith. Have you ever noticed that the Nicene Creed (link in the For Further Reading section) is nothing more than a clarification of 1 Corinthians 15:3–5, and that words directly from that Corinthian letter are built right into the Creed? (See McKnight, *King Jesus Gospel*.)

That means the gospel tells the story of Israel as it comes to fulfillment in the story of Jesus—his life, his teachings, his miracles, his death, his resurrection, his ascension, his return. The gospel also tells the story of the amazing and endless benefits of the gospel, and you can pick your terms: salvation, redemption, liberation, justification, forgiveness, sanctification, participation in Christ, transformation, and on and on. False teaching, for Paul, distracts from the gospel, as it substitutes for Christ, diminishes faith, and degrades the benefits that come to us by God's grace, not our own doings. Notice how Paul reminds Timothy of the value of faith in the gospel: "advancing God's work—which is by faith" (1:4) and "a sincere faith" (1:5).

Leaders lead with this gospel—the gospel about Jesus, appropriated by faith, and has amazing benefits and only by faith and only through Jesus—and those who know this gospel recognize when it gets corrupted. Some are tempted to think that their favorite idea or brand of theology constitutes the gospel and that any variation from that idea of theology is heresy. Equating one's political party with God's party is like scratching the surface of a chalkboard with a fingernail. And the next thing you know, the gospel is America. This can be idolatry, and it can be heresy. But the standard of measurement is the gospel, and the gospel alone.

So please get the gospel right and latch onto it for all your nourishment.

Studying the Gospel

Read and study 1 Corinthians 15:1–28; 2 Timothy 2:8–12; Acts 2; 10–11; 13–14; The Gospels.

Bates, Matthew. *Gospel Allegiance: What Faith in Jesus Misses for Salvation in Christ*. Grand Rapids: Brazos, 2019.

McKnight, Scot. *The King Jesus Gospel: The Original Good News Revisited*. Rev. ed. Grand Rapids: Zondervan, 2016.

Wright, N. T. *What Saint Paul Really Said*. 2nd ed. Grand Rapids: Eerdmans, 2014, 37–67.

LEADERS LEAD BY RECOGNIZING CORRUPTIONS OF THE GOSPEL

The most common corruption of the gospel Paul faced, and that Timothy needed to deal with, was mixing the gospel with the law of Moses. Everywhere the apostle preached and planted a church, chaos eventually ensued over whether gentile converts were to follow the law of Moses or not.

Take a quick look at Acts 13:45, 50; 14:2, 4–7. Then read Galatians and Romans 14–15. That's all it takes to recognize the problem Paul faced. There were good reasons Paul was facing problems. Paul was a recognized Jewish leader with plenty of connections with the rabbis back in Jerusalem. But he was teaching that gentiles did not have to follow the law to be in Christ. Faith was enough; baptism was enough.

Imagine Jewish believers, or Jewish unbelievers, watching Paul and asking, "Don't you believe the law of Moses is God's Word? Are you denying the authority of Scripture? Who gave you permission to say gentiles who enter into Abraham's family don't have to follow God's covenant code for God's people?" Not all agreed with Paul, and some of those who disagreed were causing a disturbance in Ephesus, so Paul instructs Timothy about this problem. Remember, the gospel leads the discussion.

Paul describes in dismissive terms—typical for that day, not so helpful in ours—the beliefs of those who think Jesus followers need to follow the law. Here are his terms: "false doctrines" and "myths and endless genealogies" and "controversial speculations" and "meaningless talk" (1:3, 4, 6). He attributes these beliefs to other leaders in the community who "want to be teachers of the law"—and here Paul knows his stuff—"but they don't know what they are talking about or what they so confidently affirm" (1:7).

What they don't seem to know is that the law is not the basis for all kinds of silly speculations and myth-making, but rather God designed it to instruct humans about what is right and wrong. In fact, Paul says it is designed for sinners and not saints (1:8–9). So emphatic is he about this that he wants them to know what the stereotypical sins look like, when measured by the law. These notorious sinners are the "lawbreakers and rebels, the ungodly and sinful, the unholy and irreligious, for those who kill their fathers or mothers, for murderers, for the sexually immoral, for those practicing homosexuality, for slave traders and liars and perjurers" (1:9–10). The law was given to reveal such sins—and more beside.

Paul ties these sins into a knot and then observes that such behaviors are out of line with "the gospel concerning the glory of the blessed God" (1:11). This knot reveals that corruptions of the gospel are both ideas and behaviors, which is why Paul wants leaders to perceive the consequences of corrupting the gospel.

LEADERS LEAD BY PERCEIVING GOSPEL CONSEQUENCES

Leaders can discern the gospel they are actually promoting by the consequences in the lives of others. Are the consequences godliness and Christian virtue, or are they competition and chaos? False teachers promote "myths and endless genealogies," which reminds me of the obsessions I experienced in the 1970s, with many concerned with charts about the rapture and the tribulation and how long it would last and the second coming and Israel and Russia and the USA. Paul says bad teachings lead to "controversial speculations" rather than "advancing God's work" (1:4).

Sound gospel teaching produces people who are known for faith and love (1:4–5), not chaos and controversies. I think about this often because of the temptations of social media to draw likes and retweets and subtweets and—say what you want—attention. I wrote about this in *James and Galatians* (pp. 49–57).

Love flows directly from three other postures: "a pure heart" and "a good conscience" and "a sincere faith" (1:5). With the word "pure" Paul jabbed the false teachers. The word could be translated "clean" or even "kosher," and by pushing it into the inner life of the heart, he makes a statement that external purity is not as valuable as internal purity, just as Jesus did (Mark 7:1–20).

Leading with the gospel is what Paul knows. He knows the blessing it is to be a gospel agent in the Roman Empire, and he knows that gospel work is a sacred trust. As he says it, God "entrusted" the gospel "to me" (1:11). The word "entrusted" is a cognate of the word "faith." The verb is *pisteuō* (believe in or trust in) and the noun is *pistis* (belief or faith, trust). Get this. In effect, Paul says "God trusted me with the gospel." Leaders who lead with the gospel know the sacredness of their calling, and they guard the gospel. It's easy to forget if we get tied up in controversies and quarrels.

QUESTIONS FOR REFLECTION AND APPLICATION

1. What is the content of the gospel message with which leaders should lead?

2. How do the gospel, and the creeds based on the gospel, set the boundaries of heresy and orthodoxy?

3. How would Paul define "false teaching"?

4. Have you ever been part of a church tradition that recites the creeds? What is your view of the creeds?

5. How was the gospel first presented to you? How does that message compare with Paul's framing of the gospel?

FOR FURTHER READING

Wikipedia. s.v. "Nicene Creed." Last modified March 5, 2023. https://en.wikipedia.org/wiki/Nicene_Creed.

McKnight, Scot. *James and Galatians*. New Testament: Everyday Bible Study Series. Grand Rapids: HarperChristian Resources, 2021.

———. *The King Jesus Gospel: The Original Good News Revisited*. Rev. ed. Grand Rapids: Zondervan, 2016.

LEADERS WITNESS

1 Timothy 1:12–20

¹² I thank Christ Jesus our Lord, who has given me strength, that he considered me trustworthy, appointing me to his service. ¹³ Even though I was once a blasphemer and a persecutor and a violent man, I was shown mercy because I acted in ignorance and unbelief. ¹⁴ The grace of our Lord was poured out on me abundantly, along with the faith and love that are in Christ Jesus.

¹⁵ Here is a trustworthy saying that deserves full acceptance: Christ Jesus came into the world to save sinners—of whom I am the worst. ¹⁶ But for that very reason I was shown mercy so that in me, the worst of sinners, Christ Jesus might display his immense patience as an example for those who would believe in him and receive eternal life. ¹⁷ Now to the King eternal, immortal, invisible, the only God, be honor and glory for ever and ever. Amen.

¹⁸ Timothy, my son, I am giving you this command in keeping with the prophecies once made about you, so that by recalling them you may fight the battle well, ¹⁹ holding on to faith and a good conscience, which some have rejected and so have suffered shipwreck with regard to the faith. ²⁰ Among them are Hymenaeus and Alexander, whom I have handed over to Satan to be taught not to blaspheme.

The first century's theory of education was this: we learn more by emulation or imitation than by information and instruction. Plato taught Aristotle, who taught the whole world philosophy. Gamaliel taught Paul, who taught Timothy. Elie Wiesel taught Ariel Burger, who wrote about all he learned from Wiesel (*Witness*). While the word "witness" (*martureō*) in the New Testament describes a verbal witness, the term itself takes on a fuller sense when it became "martyr" (*martus*). So a witness is someone who testifies with one's words and one's life. Paul witnessed everywhere he went, and at the vicious hand of Nero, he became a witness as a martyr as well. Leaders witness to the gospel—by telling their story, by telling the story of Jesus, and by defending the gospel.

LEADERS WITNESS TO THE GOSPEL

Paul approached his own conversion from different angles, depending on the audience and the purpose. In Acts 9, 22, and 26 he narrates his Damascus road experience as so powerful that not only was his life revolutionized but his theology was too. In Galatians 1 he tells his story from the angle of an independent calling to gospel the gentiles, while in Philippians 3 he magnifies his Jewish credentials to diminish them in comparison to what he discovered in Christ. In today's passage we discover another way to tell his story: the witness of a sinner (1:12–17).

First Timothy's witness to his life seems almost the opposite of Philippians 3, where he emphasized his own law-abiding righteousness. Here he turns the lens onto his sinfulness. His terms are that he "was once a blasphemer and a persecutor and a violent man" (1:13; see Acts 8:1–3). He softens the blow a bit with "I acted in ignorance and unbelief"

(1 Timothy 1:13), but the impact remains: "Christ Jesus came into the world to save sinners—of whom I am the worst" and "me, the worst of sinners" (1:15, 16).

Evangelical Christians especially love a dramatic conversion story, the bigger the better. The tendency, if one is truthful, is because such stories confirm the faith of the faithful. Such stories, like Chuck Colson's or Rosaria Butterfield's, too often become a pat on one's own back. Paul's own story is both dramatic and unlike this pat-on-the-back tendency. He begins and ends his story by witnessing not to himself but to Jesus: "I thank Christ Jesus our Lord" because he empowered Paul and "considered" him worthy of trust. It was Jesus who appointed him to become a gospel-leading agent (1:12). It was "the grace of our Lord" that was "poured out" on Paul uberabundantly, and accompanying grace were the virtues of "faith and love" that came to him "in Christ Jesus" (1:14). It was "Jesus Christ" who saves sinners (1:15). The depths of sin prove in Paul's witness that Jesus wanted to "display his immense patience as an example" for those who come to believe through him (1:16). All of which erupts into glorifying God (1:17).

Notice then that Paul's own story is not actually his story but the story of the goodness and mercy and grace of God in the face of Jesus Christ. Conversion stories are a zero-sum game. The more pats we get on the back and the more claps we get for our stories, the less glory goes to God and the less praise is given to Jesus. Isn't it perverse to be applauded for how sinful we were? Leaders lead with a gospel story that magnifies Jesus Christ.

LEADERS WITNESS FOR THE GOSPEL

Those who lead with the gospel become witnesses *for* the gospel in defending the gospel and going to battle for it.

Timothy's sage, Paul, instructs him on the basis of a supernatural, prophetic beginning to his calling to be a gospel agent with Paul to "fight the battle well" (1:18). The Greek is dense. Literally it reads "that you soldier in them with beautiful soldiering" (my translation), with "in them" referring to the prophecies over Timothy. Gospel-soldiering requires "holding on to faith and a good conscience" (1:19; see 1:5 too). That is, gospel leaders are to strive to do the right thing at the right time with the right motive so their conscience can witness in them that they are glorifying Christ.

Now Paul turns the corner to specify again the problem with false teaching. Some, instead of soldiering on in the faith, have jumped ship and wandered into deep, drowning waters (1:19). Paul names them: "Hymenaeus and Alexander" (1:20). Hymenaeus denied the resurrection (2 Timothy 2:18). Paul has disciplined them in the strongest of terms: "whom I have handed over to Satan to be taught not to blaspheme" (1 Timothy 1:20). Alexander, who is probably the Jewish fellow in Acts 19:33, did some kind of harm to Paul (2 Timothy 4:14). We don't know exactly what Paul meant by "handed over to Satan," but one good guess is that these two men have been excommunicated from the assembly of believers. Paul's intent, noticeably, is not punishment or vindictiveness but the hope of restoration. The only commentary needed on this is from Paul's second letter to Timothy, which reads, "Opponents must be gently instructed, in the hope that God will grant them repentance leading them to a knowledge of the truth, and that they will come to their senses and escape from the trap of the devil, who has taken them captive to do his will" (2:25–26).

Leaders witness for the gospel, not only by telling their story but also by defending the gospel and disciplining, as well as discipling, the mistaken back into the boat.

QUESTIONS FOR REFLECTION AND APPLICATION

1. In what ways do leaders serve as witnesses?

2. How does 1 Timothy's telling of Paul's story differ from his other narrations of his story?

3. How does Paul's witnessing work intersect with his defending the gospel from false teachers?

4. Have you ever tried to correct false teaching in a church? How did that experience go?

5. How could you tell your life story in a way that gives glory to the Lord Jesus?

FOR FURTHER READING

Burger, Ariel. *Witness: Lessons from Elie Wiesel's Classroom*. Boston: Houghton Mifflin Harcourt, 2018.

LEADERS NURTURE PRAYER FOR POLITICIANS

1 Timothy 2:1–10

¹ I urge, then, first of all, that petitions, prayers, intercession and thanksgiving be made for all people—² for kings and all those in authority, that we may live peaceful and quiet lives in all godliness and holiness. ³ This is good, and pleases God our Savior, ⁴ who wants all people to be saved and to come to a knowledge of the truth. ⁵ For there is one God and one mediator between God and mankind, the man Christ Jesus, ⁶ who gave himself as a ransom for all people. This has now been witnessed to at the proper time. ⁷ And for this purpose I was appointed a herald and an apostle—I am telling the truth, I am not lying—and a true and faithful teacher of the Gentiles.

⁸ Therefore I want the men everywhere to pray, lifting up holy hands without anger or disputing. ⁹ I also want the women to dress modestly, with decency and propriety, adorning themselves, not with elaborate hairstyles or gold or pearls or expensive clothes, ¹⁰ but with good deeds, appropriate for women who profess to worship God.

At times the apostle Paul is like a speaker who clearly begins a topic, wanders a bit off topic to clarify something, and only vaguely returns to the original topic. That's what happens in today's passage. Both verse 1 and 8 make it clear Paul is talking about prayer. Both paragraphs, however, seem to create their own little sidebars (vv. 4–7, vv. 9–10). So if you had a bit of trouble following Paul, he wanted you instead to follow him where he was going.

When Paul says "first of all," he means that socially respectable Christian practice requires praying for one's community and not just for oneself, one's family, or one's house church. The kind of prayer he has in mind spans the prayer life: petitionary prayer, generic prayers (synagogues in the Diaspora were called "houses of prayer"), intercessory prayers, and prayers of gratitude to God.

LEADERS NURTURE PRAYER
FOR ALL PEOPLE

Paul urged prayer for "all people." In our church we pray publicly every Sunday for the church worldwide, for the mission of the church to spread the gospel, for peace in the world, for the poor and persecuted and sick and those who suffer, for our own congregation, for our enemies, and for ourselves. Whatever the Lord brings to mind, pray for that.

LEADERS NURTURE PRAYER
FOR POLITICIANS

The earliest Christians grew in both perception and relationship to the political authorities in the Roman Empire, some of whom were brutal to them. Yet the apostle Paul expects local leaders to lead in praying "for kings [or emperors] and all those in authority," and the reason for the prayer was to promote "godliness and holiness" and to protect the church from social foolishness. The word "godliness" has recently taken on fresh insights through the research of Christopher Hoklotubbe, who has shown in his academic study that the term *eusebeia* is the Greek equivalent of the Latin *pietas*. Not only that, but those terms referred to the public practice of one's religion in a manner that was socially respectable (Hoklotubbe, *Civilized Piety*; McKnight, "*Eusebeia*"). Put directly, we are to pray for the political leaders, and we are also to live the kind of life that is socially respectable—that is, instead of living in anarchy and rebellion. This was the most common strategy of Christians in the early church. However, as the Book of Revelation shows, at times they had to resist as dissidents of the empire because nonresistance was complicity in sin. Socially respectable public practice of one's faith, however, did not mean some kind of bland acceptance of the religions of the empire. No, there was a "sly civility" at work in the Christians' public behaviors.

Sly Civility

The author of the Pastorals attempts to portray Christians as civilized and exemplary participants within the Roman social order who nevertheless maintained their theological distinctiveness (which, of course, could be considered "countercultural" in its own respect), representing a singular strategic response of what might be considered a "sly civility" along a spectrum of early Christian attempts to negotiate their imperial situation (Hoklotubbe, *Civilized Piety*, 216).

One of the traditions of the American church has been the development of prayers for the president and for the people, and I include now two such prayers from *The Book of Common Prayer*. Prayers like these are found in many church prayer books.

O Lord our Governor, whose glory is in all the world: We commend this nation to *thy* merciful care, that, being guided by *thy* Providence, we may dwell secure in *thy* peace. Grant to the President of the United States, the Governor of this State (*or* Commonwealth), and to all in authority, wisdom and strength to know and to do *thy* will. Fill them with the love of truth and righteousness, and make them ever mindful of their calling to serve this people in *thy* fear; through Jesus Christ our Lord, who *liveth* and *reigneth* with *thee* and the Holy Spirit, one God, world without end. *Amen.* (*The Book of Common Prayer*, 820)

Lord God Almighty, you have made all the peoples of the earth for your glory, to serve you in freedom and in peace: Give to the people of our country a zeal for justice and the strength of forbearance, that we may use our liberty in accordance with your gracious will; through Jesus Christ our Lord, who lives and reigns with you and the Holy Spirit, one God, for ever and ever. *Amen.* (*The Book of Common Prayer*, 258)

I believe every American church should publicly pray every Sunday for the president and for the people. I also know for many people any current president could raise one's blood pressure. If we practice this every Sunday forever and a day, we will learn to pray even, and especially, for the presidents we don't like.

Why? Because it is "good, and pleases God our Savior" (2:3). Full stop. But Paul goes on: the God who is pleased with our various prayers for politicians "wants all people to be saved and to come to a knowledge of the truth" (2:4). This is where Paul creates his own little sidebar. He says our God wants all to embrace Jesus in faith and allegiance because, contrary to the idols and temples and shrines all around them, "there is one God and one mediator," Jesus, and he "gave himself a ransom for all people" (2:5–6). Continuing his sidebar with a sidebar in a sidebar, Paul notes again the sacred trust given to him to be an agent of the gospel to gentiles (2:7).

LEADERS NURTURE PRAYER BEHAVIORS

Now back to leaders praying when they assemble. In public prayers Paul asks one thing for men and one thing for women. Paul wants the men to pray, which is expressed in the postures in which they prayed, "lifting up holy hands" in a socially respectable manner: "without anger or disputing" (2:8). I find that one interesting, and every time I read it, I wonder if the men of that time had anger issues. Yes, just look at Romans 12:19 and 14:1, as well as at James 1:19–21 and 4:1–2. Some things never change.

Paul, it is usually assumed, wants the women to avoid the appearance of opulence and thus also of shaming the poor by showing off their high-status clothing. So he exhorts them to dress "modestly" because it expresses Christian character but also social equality for all believers. They are to be known for "good deeds" far more than their fine clothing (2:9–10).

This traditional teaching about female modesty deserves a more careful explanation. Based on my forthcoming commentary on the Pastoral Epistles, I quote with light editing the rest of this paragraph: One is led by the concentration of words about respect to the conclusion that the assemblies were getting tied into flouting wealth among Christians in Ephesus. However, the language about so-called modest clothing urges the women to dress in a manner *communicating civilized piety as Christians understood such piety*. The word "modestly" concerns their "worldly fashionable outfits," or one could translate this as "I want them to face the world in worldly clothing"— but not in the sense of sinful worldliness. (The word "world" can mean "fashionable" or "decorous.") Notice now what is being said: Paul offers instruction for the Christian women *to keep status and social location in mind in how they dress*, but also with "decency and propriety." These two terms have a woman's and the church's social location in mind. Not below social custom, not above it. Behind the word "decency" is *aidous*, while behind "propriety" is *sōphrosynēs*, terms that could be rendered "with dignity and class" or "with respect," while the second term could be understood as "with prudence" or "good sense" and even "with public self-control" (cf. 2:15).

Domestic Virtues

From an inscription written by a man about his wife at the turn of the first century, the husband of his now-deceased wife after forty-one years of marriage refers to her in these terms: "As for your domestic virtues, loyalty (to our marriage), obedience, courteousness, easy good-nature, your assiduous wool-working, reverence (for the gods) without superstition, attire not designed for attracting attention, modest refinement— what need have I to make mention of these?" (G. H. R. Horsley, *New Documents Illustrating Early Christianity* 3 [Grand Rapids: Eerdmans, 1983], 34)

All this to say that we have, on the basis of one kind of reading of these instructions for women, almost pushed women into the world of the Amish and Old Order Mennonites (no disrespect to them) and missed the very point Paul is making. This is not an injunction for women to dress backward, nor does it instruct them into some form of asceticism. Rather, Paul urges the women to wear socially respectable clothing. Both culture and social location determine what clothing to wear.

Leaders lead the church by guiding for whom it prays and how the people praying conduct themselves. Let me give a piece of advice about the conduct called clothing: be careful what you say. I'm of an age that I cannot for the life of me understand why some men wear stocking caps during the whole service. When I grew up, men wore to church dress hats (with feathered decorations in the band), and we put them on the coat rack. If I'd have worn one during the service, my mother or father—probably mother—would have taken me outside the sanctuary and told me to take it off. If I wore such a hat today, I'd be out of step with what is socially respectable. But no one would care. I'll leave the topic of clothing right there.

QUESTIONS FOR REFLECTION AND APPLICATION

1. What instruction for prayer does Paul give in this passage?

2. How does praying for political leaders impact local churches?

3. In what ways does this passage convey Paul's concern that the churches be socially respectable?

4. Does your church include public prayer in your gatherings? What do you pray for together?

5. What have you been taught by the church about modest dress? How has this explanation impacted your understanding of Paul's guidance?

FOR FURTHER READING

McKnight, Scot. "*Eusebeia* as Social Respectability: The Public Life of the Christian Pastor." Pages 157–74 in *Rhetoric, History, and Theology: Interpreting the New Testament*. Edited by Todd D. Still and Jason A. Meyers. Lanham, MD: Lexington/Fortress Academic, 2021.

LEADERS NURTURE THEOLOGICAL EDUCATION

1 Timothy 2:11–15

[11] A woman should learn in quietness and full submission. [12] I do not permit a woman to teach or to assume authority over a man; she must be quiet. [13] For Adam was formed first, then Eve. [14] And Adam was not the one deceived; it was the woman who was deceived and became a sinner. [15] But women will be saved through childbearing—if they continue in faith, love and holiness with propriety.

When you read a passage in the Bible, like this one, that seems to butt up against what you expected to read, it's always a good idea to poke around in the rest of that book of the Bible to see if it might give some context. If you approached this passage, as many before you have done, knowing that God has always used women to lead— think of Deborah in Judges or Huldah in 2 Kings 22:14 and 2 Chronicles 34:22, where the priest, Hilkiah, chose to consult first with the female prophet, or think of Mary or Junia the apostle or Priscilla, a teacher (Acts 18:26; cf. Titus 2:3), or women prophets (1 Corinthians 11:5), the daughters of Philip (Acts 21:9), and women praying publicly in Corinth. Knowing this minimal list of women active in leading, speaking, praying, and prophesying, you may be surprised by how tight Paul's words sound.

That's why we need to turn a page or two to 1 Timothy 5, where we read about some women who seem to be a bit troublesome for the church in Ephesus. A city known for high-class women, by the way. A city that worshiped in one of the seven wonders of the ancient world, the Temple of Artemis. A city known for attracting intelligent, philosophical women. Here are the verses I am thinking of in chapter 5:

> As for younger widows, do not put them on such a list. For when their sensual desires overcome their dedication to Christ, they want to marry. Thus they bring judgment on themselves, because they have broken their first pledge. Besides, they get into the habit of being idle and going about from house to house. And not only do they become idlers, but also busybodies who talk nonsense, saying things they ought not to. So I counsel younger widows to marry, to have children, to manage their homes and to give the enemy no opportunity for slander. Some have in fact already turned away to follow Satan. (5:11–15)

We will discuss this passage when we get to it, but for now just notice that these women are said to be socialites, for moving about from house to house (an upper-class thing), they are idlers, and they "talk nonsense, saying things they ought not to." These are probably the same women who were using their clothing to make status, if not also perhaps sexualized, statements (2:9–10). These are the women about whom Paul is speaking in 2:11–15. For such women, Paul has a message for the leaders.

EDUCATE

It is a conceit of men to orient all their thoughts on the words "quietness and full submission"—he's talking here about civilized piety again—and "I do not permit a woman to teach" and "quiet" when the operative word here is "learn," a word connected to the word "disciple." Paul wants these women to be discipled and, in the period of their discipleship, not to be talking "nonsense." First, teach these women the rudiments of the gospel and theology and morality. Paul outlines the message one chapter later (3:15–16). The evidence of the letters of Paul about women does not suggest total silence, but there is a time for silence until a woman has been catechized into the faith.

A well-known pastor and professor of future pastors and theologians, Helmut Thielicke, once said, "During the period when the voice is changing, we do not sing, and during this formative period in the life of the theological student" such a student, he concludes, "does not preach" (Thielicke, *Little Exercise*, 31–32). Why? Not ready. That's what Paul is saying in 1 Timothy 2. He cannot have meant women are never to talk in church, because women talked in Paul's churches!

THE PROBLEM

Paul states the problem here, and the NIV translation is "assume authority" (2:12). The term comes from the lexicon of power and suggests women of wealth and power and network who can "overwhelm" or even "usurp authority" over the men leading in the house churches of Ephesus. Such women need to be educated, so Paul exhorts Timothy to make sure of some theological education for these wealthy, intelligent, influential women.

A FALSE TEACHING

You may know there is more than a little discussion about these verses, and at times one can feel like one is running on a hamster wheel. In Ephesus perhaps a teaching was running around that believed women were created first. So Paul makes a double point: (1) No, Adam was created first and (2) Eve was the first one to be deceived. Maybe then what Paul is saying is not that women are more easily deceived but that women can lead others astray (again, the women of 1 Timothy 5 who need to be educated, as in 2:11). Women, Paul goes on, don't need to pursue a life of asceticism and sexual denial—Paul speaks of this at 4:3—but they can marry and find redemption through the protection of Israel's God (2:15). All the leader needs to concentrate on is discipleship in the direction of "faith, love and holiness with propriety" (2:15).

THE HAMSTER WHEEL

So let me spin that hamster wheel a little more. What if, instead, Paul is writing about a wife's relationship to her husband? The Greek word for "woman" and "man" are the same words for "wife" and "husband." Only the context tells us. Does it here? Perhaps, but I do think the younger widows of 1 Timothy 5:11 are a clearer text for the women of 1 Timothy 2:11. In which case, the words are not for a wife and husband but for a specific group of women in Ephesus who need education.

QUESTIONS FOR REFLECTION
AND APPLICATION

1. How does 1 Timothy 5 help interpret 1 Timothy 2 on the issue of women teaching in the church?

2. What are church leaders to do about educating and discipling the church women?

3. Why does Paul bring up Adam and Eve here?

4. How does knowing what other letters from Paul said women were free to do impact your reading of this letter?

5. How have you been taught to interpret this passage in the past? How has this interpretation impacted your view?

FOR FURTHER READING

I have avoided citations and quotations, but here is a brief list of recommended readings about women in church ministries:

Cohick, Lynn. *Women in the World of the Earliest Christians: Illuminating Ancient Ways of Life.* Grand Rapids: Baker Academic, 2009, 138–40.

Glahn, Sandra L. "The First-Century Ephesian Artemis: Ramifications of Her Identity." *Bibliotheca Sacra* 172, no. 688 (October 2015): 450–69.

———. "The Identity of Artemis in First-Century Ephesus." *Bibliotheca Sacra* 172, no. 687 (July 2015): 316–34.

McKnight, Scot. *The Blue Parakeet: Rethinking How You Read the Bible.* 2nd ed. Grand Rapids: Zondervan, 2018, 245–48, 285–88.

Thielicke, Helmut. *A Little Exercise for Young Theologians.* Grand Rapids: Eerdmans, 2016.

Towner, Philip H. *The Letters to Timothy and Titus.* New International Critical Commentary. Grand Rapids: Eerdmans, 2006, 212–39.

LEADERS NURTURE LEADERS, PART 1

1 Timothy 3:1–7

*¹ Here is a trustworthy saying: Whoever aspires to be an overseer
desires a noble task. ² Now the overseer is to be above reproach,
faithful to his wife, temperate, self-controlled, respectable, hospitable, able to teach, ³ not given to drunkenness, not violent but gentle,
not quarrelsome, not a lover of money. ⁴ He must manage his own
family well and see that his children obey him, and he must do so
in a manner worthy of full respect. ⁵ (If anyone does not know how
to manage his own family, how can he take care of God's church?)
⁶ He must not be a recent convert, or he may become conceited and
fall under the same judgment as the devil. ⁷ He must also have a
good reputation with outsiders, so that he will not fall into disgrace
and into the devil's trap.*

Paul writes to another pastor-leader named Titus, and no
sooner has he spelled out his customary greetings than
he instructs Titus to "appoint elders in every town" on the
island of Crete (Titus 1:5). In this letter, having to deal with
false teachings in Ephesus, Paul doesn't get to that part of
Timothy's task until chapter 3, but finding leaders for the
churches was uppermost on his mind. The words Paul uses in

1 Timothy 3 are "overseer" (3:1), which is perhaps best translated as "mentor," and then "deacons" (3:8) and then probably women deacons or women mentors in 3:11.

Good leaders tend to fill the gap between their tenure and the next group of leaders. They fill the gap by discerning future leaders and mentoring those leaders. Only a deeply insecure leader resists the impulse to tend to that gap. The unstated principle at work in today's passage is the discipling or mentoring ministry of the "overseer."

More than that, good leaders pastor or mentor people to be more like Christ. Barbara Brown Taylor, speaking of the impact of her own pastor on her to become a pastor, once said, "He seemed able, when he looked at me, to see a person and not only a child, and I loved him for it" (Taylor, *The Preaching Life*, 15). People make up a church, and not the people we by and large choose, but the people who gather there. Only over time do they become friends and siblings. The pastor's calling is to pastor those she's got, not those she'd like to get, which means pastoring is complicated because humans are complicated. Very much so at times. But today's passage is about finding the next generation of leaders, so we turn to finding and nurturing leaders.

LET'S START WITH ARISTOTLE

A person was judged in the ancient world by virtue, which was a person's character as it was formed on the basis of practicing good habits over time—in the context, of course, of close relations with others with good character. No one was more influential on defining virtue than the philosopher Aristotle. Here is a list of the virtues Aristotle taught in his famous book *Nicomachean Ethics*. Please read through each of these as he describes the ideal "mean" between a deficiency and an excess.

Deficiency	The Mean	Excess
1. Coward	Courage	Rash
2. Unable to feel	Temperance	Intemperance
3. Lack of generosity	Generosity	Profligacy
4. Pettiness	Magnificence	Vulgarity
5. Pusillanimity	Magnanimity	Vanity
6. Unambitious	Good ambition	Bad ambition
7. Passivity	Gentleness	Irascibility
8. Self-deprecation	Truthfulness	Boastfulness
9. Boorishness	Wit	Buffoonery
10. Quarrelsomeness	Friendliness	Obsequious
11. Bad-tempered	Friendliness [same as 10]	Flatterer
12. Shameless	Polite	Bashful
13. Spitefulness	Righteous indignation	Enviousness

Now, let's compare Paul's two lists in 1 Timothy 3 and Titus 1:

1 Timothy 3:1–7, numbered and abbreviated:

The overseer is

1. to be above reproach,
2. faithful to his wife,
3. temperate,
4. self-controlled,
5. respectable,
6. hospitable,
7. able to teach,
8. not given to drunkenness,
9. not violent but gentle,
10. not quarrelsome,
11. not a lover of money.
12. He must manage his own family well and see that his children obey him, and he must do so in a manner worthy of full respect. . . .
13. He must not be a recent convert . . .
14. He must also have a good reputation with outsiders.

The following list is Titus 1:6–9 for comparison, numbered, abbreviated. Please notice "elder" instead of "overseer" to begin the passage, but it shifts to "overseer" at verse 7. The distinction between these two ministries is not always clear in the early church period.

An elder must be

1. blameless,
2. faithful to his wife,
3. a man whose children believe and are not open to the charge of being wild and disobedient.
4. Since an overseer manages God's household, he must be

5. blameless—not overbearing, not quick-tempered,
6. not given to drunkenness,
7. not violent,
8. not pursuing dishonest gain.
9. Rather, he must be hospitable,
10. one who loves what is good,
11. who is self-controlled,
12. upright,
13. holy
14. and disciplined.
15. He must hold firmly to the trustworthy message as it has been taught, so that he can encourage others by sound doctrine and refute those who oppose it.

LEADERS KNOW THAT LISTS ONLY DO SO MUCH

Aristotle's list fascinates me because he focused so much on character. Sadly, many have turned away from understanding Paul's two lists as signs of character to thinking of them as a job description or a list of skills or, worse yet, a magical checklist of easily identifiable marks in a person.

Two observations. First, Paul's lists in Titus and in 1 Timothy 3 are not identical because his lists were not skills or a job description. He wasn't thinking of a required checklist of qualifications. Paul saw these items as *indications of a person's Christian character and maturity in discipleship.* Because the lists aren't the same in the two different letters, and the letters were written probably at about the same time, we should avoid adding them up into a master list or reducing them to common denominators. Instead, we need to perceive them as indicators of character. Overall, a leader should be a "good character" or "mature Christian" or a "committed disciple of Jesus."

Second, just as Aristotle's list expresses what he saw as necessary to lead a city in ancient Greece, so Paul's list communicates those traits he had learned were needed to lead house churches in the Roman Empire in the first century. These are experience-based virtues for pastoral ministry. Centuries have changed the experiences, and the traits needed for pastoral leadership have adjusted into all their many varieties today. After all, who has a church ministry today without a worship leader and musicians and vocalists? And most churches to this day believe pastors need seminary or at least some theological training. Those traits are at best either invisible or barely visible in Paul's lists.

LEADERS KNOW CHRISTIAN LEADERSHIP IS DISTINCT

Notice the middle line of Aristotle's list—the so-called golden mean—and compare that with the character traits in 1 Timothy 3. Aristotle's top character marks are courage, temperance, generosity, magnificence, magnanimity, good ambition, gentleness, truthfulness, wit, friendliness, polite, and righteous indignation. Paul baptizes virtues in the ancient world, both Greco-Roman and (don't forget) Jewish, to draw attention to the following, and I now synthesize his list:

- Socially respectable: both publicly and at home
- Faithful to one's wife—or a one-woman man
- Controlled: socially, in drinking, emotionally, with money
- Hospitable
- Teachable or able to teach
- Discipled

Put simply, the core character traits just mentioned fit well into what is socially respectable in the Greco-Roman world, and such people would stand up well with those in Aristotle's tradition. A noticeable theme in the Pastoral Epistles is the theme of civilized piety or a socially respectable life. Paul learned from experience that the church leaders and churches did best when they behaved. One might factor in, too, that he had learned this as a Jew in the city of Tarsus because Jews learned how to live in the Diaspora.

The theme of a socially respectable life deserves more attention in churches today. A socially respectable life is earned over time when others observe character, wisdom, social conscience, justice, and fair-mindedness (McKnight, "*Eusebeia*"). The witness of a local church is most hurt by greedy leaders, abusive pastors, socially unengaged elders—in other words, the development of a bad or selfish or self-centered reputation. A pastor friend of mine went to the local school board and asked a simple question: "What can our church do to help your school?" The chair of the school board said to him, "We've never had a church ask us that. They've only asked what we can do for them." That church helped bring a school up to local codes, and that church's witness made the whole church socially respectable.

But *socially* respectable is not all Paul cares about. Paul's virtues shift the focus from the public forum to house churches. Each of these character traits receives a re-formation in the Jewish and Christian tradition. The primary social location for these traits is not the public forum but the house church, though the forum ought to be able to observe these traits too. Instead, the house church becomes the schoolroom in which new believers are mentored into Christian character, and virtuous people carry their virtues into the public forum, where they become socially respectable.

QUESTIONS FOR REFLECTION
AND APPLICATION

1. What is Paul's concern for future leaders in the churches he planted?

2. How do Paul's recommended character traits compare to Aristotle's?

3. List your top five qualities or character traits you think are most important for a church leader. How do they compare to Paul's list?

4. Who were your mentors? What did you learn from them? To whom can you be more intentional about offering mentoring?

5. Are your church leaders socially respectable? Why or why not?

FOR FURTHER READING

Brown Taylor, Barbara. *The Preaching Life: Living Out Your Vocation*. Lanham, MD: Cowley, 1993.

McKnight, Scot. "*Eusebeia* as Social Respectability: The Public Life of the Christian Pastor." Pages 157–74 in *Rhetoric, History, and Theology: Interpreting the New Testament*. Edited by Todd D. Still and Jason A. Meyers. Lanham, MD: Lexington/Fortress Academic, 2021.

LEADERS NURTURE LEADERS, PART 2

1 Timothy 3:8–13

⁸ In the same way, deacons are to be worthy of respect, sincere, not indulging in much wine, and not pursuing dishonest gain. ⁹ They must keep hold of the deep truths of the faith with a clear conscience. ¹⁰ They must first be tested; and then if there is nothing against them, let them serve as deacons.

¹¹ In the same way, the women are to be worthy of respect, not malicious talkers but temperate and trustworthy in everything.

¹² A deacon must be faithful to his wife and must manage his children and his household well. ¹³ Those who have served well gain an excellent standing and great assurance in their faith in Christ Jesus.

Our view of how early churches were structured on an org chart is clouded by some mists of not knowing, but this seems to be the best we can know: there were apostles and prophets and evangelists who were not located in one church so much as agents on the move. Local house churches had pastoral leaders who were called overseers, elders, and deacons. Not all were men—Junia is an apostle mentioned in Romans 16:7—and one might even suggest there was an official group of leaders called "widows" (1 Timothy 5:3–16).

Deacons

The overlap between the virtues of an overseer (3:1) and a "deacon" (3:8) are substantial, so much so that one can be forgiven if one thinks of deacons as younger folks who someday may become overseers. Perhaps, but what is clear is that the virtues mentioned for a deacon (3:8–10) are also the virtues of the socially respectable. Which is precisely how Paul begins: "worthy of respect," though the NIV adds "worthy of" (3:8). Six more elements of a leaderly character now come into view.

First, with "sincere" Paul uses a graphic word, which could be translated "double-worded," or what today is called speaking with a forked tongue—that is, affirming a person to their face but discrediting the same person to other people. Second, experience taught Paul that leaders need to control their drinking of alcohol, and here it is "wine." (The Bible does not teach teetotalism but self-control. Those who can't control their drinking can be advised to teetotalism.) Third, starting with Jesus and sprouting wings in the earliest churches was a clear commitment to avoid the selfishness of greed and consumption as one became generous and giving for those in need. So leaders were taught not to be "pursuing dishonest gain," an older term for which was "avaricious." Paul again uses a graphic word: *aischrokerdēs*. It means "ugliness" or "sordidness" in one's pursuit of "gain" or "accumulation." Think of Jacob Marley and Ebenezer Scrooge in Charles Dickens's *A Christmas Carol* and you've got your character types.

Fourth, Timothy's search for deacons will include finding

people who grip "the deep truths" (the word is "mystery") "of the faith" in such a manner that they are never "double-worded" about it: what they publicly affirm when they recited the creed, they believe in their bones (3:9). What Paul means by "deep truths" is not about the rapture or infant baptism or the time of a church service on Sunday. The mystery in Pauline letters will be spelled out in 3:16, where it gets the header of "the mystery from which true godliness springs." In one word, the mystery is the gospel: Jesus appeared, was vindicated in his resurrection, was seen by angels, was preached in the world, was trusted, and was "taken up in glory." A basic character trait for a deacon is affirmation of that gospel.

Fifth, Timothy is to search for deacons who have been through what an old man in my childhood church, by the name of Pop Brubaker, called "the school of hard knocks." In Paul's words, deacons "must first be tested," that is, they've demonstrated over time their ability to be faithful in conduct and beliefs (3:10).

WOMEN

Now a little twist by Paul. Appearing as it does between instructions to men, this instruction to women in 3:11 perhaps refers to the wives of deacons. However, Paul does not say a word about the wives of overseers in 3:1–7, and he elsewhere calls Phoebe a deacon (Romans 16:1–2). By saying "In the same way," Paul logically parallels "women" to the male "deacons" of 1 Timothy 3:8, and he does not write *their* wives but simply has "women." Timothy is to include virtuous women in the circle of virtuous men who have the character traits of a deacon. In Christ there is no longer "male and female" (Galatians 3:28).

The traits of these women deacons in 1 Timothy 3:11 are, like the men, (1) "worthy of respect," (2) not slanderers,

(3) moderate in their behaviors and style of communication, and (4) allegiant to Jesus Christ in all their ways. One more time, this all adds up to a socially respectable way of life, whether it is a man or woman, and if they have that way of life, they are welcomed into the circle of overseers and deacons.

More on Deacons

Sixth, as with the overseers, the deacon is to be "faithful to his wife" (3:12) (again, the "one-woman-man" is a more literal translation), which can be flipped now that we have seen women deacons, to a woman being faithful to her husband. Home life matters, and Paul expects all the leaders—overseers, elders, deacons—to lead the home by discipling everyone to follow Christ, both in the home and in the public sector (3:12). It is a fact known to many that children of some church leaders abandon the faith. If these traits mentioned for overseers and elders are turned into a rigid checklist, such church leaders would have to be removed. But these are not a rigid list of necessary, inflexible qualifications, but rather manifestations of an experience-based kind of character needed for respectable leadership. You have heard this many times, but what Paul expects of leaders in his lists is not reserved for leaders. Everything he tells them here he will instruct for all believers in other locations. The difference is that he has a stronger expectation of these virtues for leaders.

And that's why Paul finishes off with, "Those who have served [cognate to "deacon"] well *gain an excellent standing*" (3:13, emphasis added), or as I prefer, "secure for themselves a beautiful status," which points us once again to what is socially respectable. Such people gain the capacity to speak the gospel into the lives of others. The NIV's "great assurance" translates a Greek term used for "frank speech" by those in a trusted relationship (3:13). Paul does not refer here to what one senses internally but what one can do confidently in the public sector. People of virtue gain credibility and the platform to speak their mind.

QUESTIONS FOR REFLECTION AND APPLICATION

1. How are deacons different from overseers/elders? How are they the same?

2. What leadership roles might women have played in Paul's churches?

3. Why is the social respectability of Christians so important to Paul?

4. How does your church or denomination structure church leadership? What are the qualifications for various church leaders?

5. If Timothy were to look at your life according to Paul's guidance, how might he evaluate your giftedness and preparation for church leadership?

LEADERS LEAD
WITH THE BASICS

1 Timothy 3:14–4:16

14 Although I hope to come to you soon, I am writing you these instructions so that, 15 if I am delayed, you will know how people ought to conduct themselves in God's household, which is the church of the living God, the pillar and foundation of the truth. 16 Beyond all question, the mystery from which true godliness springs is great:

> *He appeared in the flesh,*
>   *was vindicated by the Spirit,*
> *was seen by angels,*
>   *was preached among the nations,*
> *was believed on in the world,*
>   *was taken up in glory.*

4:1 The Spirit clearly says that in later times some will abandon the faith and follow deceiving spirits and things taught by demons. 2 Such teachings come through hypocritical liars, whose consciences have been seared as with a hot iron. 3 They forbid people to marry and order them to abstain from certain foods, which God created to be received with thanksgiving by those who believe and who know the truth. 4 For everything God created is good, and nothing is to be rejected if it is received with thanksgiving, ⁵ because it is consecrated by the word of God and prayer.

⁶ If you point these things out to the brothers and sisters, you will be a good minister of Christ Jesus, nourished on the truths of the faith and of the good teaching that you have followed. ⁷ Have nothing to do with godless myths and old wives' tales; rather, train yourself to be godly. ⁸ For physical training is of some value, but godliness has value for all things, holding promise for both the present life and the life to come. ⁹ This is a trustworthy saying that deserves full acceptance. ¹⁰ That is why we labor and strive, because we have put our hope in the living God, who is the Savior of all people, and especially of those who believe.

¹¹ Command and teach these things. ¹² Don't let anyone look down on you because you are young, but set an example for the believers in speech, in conduct, in love, in faith and in purity. ¹³ Until I come, devote yourself to the public reading of Scripture, to preaching and to teaching. ¹⁴ Do not neglect your gift, which was given you through prophecy when the body of elders laid their hands on you.

¹⁵ Be diligent in these matters; give yourself wholly to them, so that everyone may see your progress. ¹⁶ Watch your life and doctrine closely. Persevere in them, because if you do, you will save both yourself and your hearers.

Basics matter. Basics, like the coding in a computer or the discipline to arrive at work on time, are mostly hidden until you realize that the basics are missing. Think of speaking skills for a teacher, time with children for a parent, Bible knowledge for a youth group leader, driving skills for a commuter, relational skills for a pastor, administrative grit for the office manager, or perception of personality types for a human resources manager. Without them, one better get 'er done or get another job. Basics matter for the apostle Paul's vision of how Timothy needed to help local leaders. I see four basics in today's passage.

Basics of the Faith

One major basic of the Christian life centers the connection of one's behavior and one's beliefs. One can understand and believe the most intricate details of orthodox Christian faith and be a toad in behavior, and one can conduct oneself in an appropriate Christian manner and believe heresies and myths. One doesn't guarantee the other, *but the two are linked as mutual responsibilities*. That linkage permits Paul first to tell Timothy to teach the churches "how people ought to conduct themselves in God's household" (3:15), and this instruction is not about how to behave inside a church building but how people who are in the family of God are to live. What would such behavior look like? Just from 1 Timothy, we would highlight love, transparent integrity, and faith (1:5), as well as prayer (2:1, 8), socially respectable living both in the assembly and in public (2:2), and holiness (2:15). Now read through the virtues of 1 Timothy 3 and you've got a grip on Paul's vision for "conduct" in 3:15.

Conduct and beliefs are mutual responsibilities of believers. The faith is broken down in 1 Timothy 3:16 in poetic lines, and some think this was either an early confession of faith or even some kind of early song sung in the assemblies. Each line is about Jesus first and foremost: he lived and died, he was raised and seen by angels at the tomb, and then the word got out by some evangelist types and people began to believe in him, and he ascended. Perhaps you have said it this way yourself, as I have many times, "The Stone Table cracked. Aslan is roaming Narnia again." What joy that story brings to children (and adults) when they read it in *The Lion, the Witch and the Wardrobe*! And what joy these lines in 1 Timothy 3:16 bring to the believer every time she hears that death could not contain him. God is, as the songwriter has it, "still rolling stones" because God rolled the stone that matters most.

That kind of life and that kind of faith are basics.

Basics of God as Creator

God designed men and women to have sex. That I just said that in this context may have surprised you, but that's the major point Paul says to Timothy in 4:1–5. Evidently some people in Ephesus were down on sex and were vigorously advocating for virginity and celibacy. It's called "asceticism." Such people "forbid people to marry and order them to abstain from certain foods" (4:3). We can't be sure who these teachers were, but perhaps they were "Hymenaeus and Alexander" (1:20) or perhaps the widows of 1 Timothy 5, or perhaps both, or perhaps neither!

The Spirit has revealed such teachings to be signs of the "later times," when some believers "will abandon the faith and follow deceiving spirits and things taught by demons" (4:1). Paul turns on the teachers of such things and labels them with bold-font labels, like "hypocritical liars," and he says their God-given "consciences" has been "seared as with a hot iron" (4:2).

We've got now what was being taught and that it was being taught by false teachers. Why was it wrong? Because, as I said, God designed men and women to have sex as well as to eat a wide variety of foods. All that God creates is good (Genesis 1 uses "good" with creation often). Both bring pleasure. Pleasure is fine, as long as it doesn't get out of hand in promiscuity and gluttony. God expects only that believers thank God for foods, and some think he's also including sex (4:3). Indulgent people overeat and oversex, and such people also do not thank God for the gifts of creation. Prayers of thanksgiving turn the Creator's gifts into gifts devoted to God (4:5).

BASICS OF CIVILIZED PIETY

At the heart of the next paragraph in today's passage is Paul's favorite theme in 1 Timothy, this time given to Timothy himself: "train yourself to be godly." Playing on the word "train," he continues with, "For physical training is of some value, but godliness has value for all things" (4:7–8), and he then says in 4:9 that "this is a trustworthy saying." In 4:7–8 we hear Paul's favorite word again. Godliness translates *eusebeia*, which in his world pointed to civilized piety or socially respectable living that gives a good reputation to the gospel and the church. Paul does not have in mind simply being a publicly nice woman or man. Paul has in mind Christian behaviors that overlap with publicly respectable behaviors but, because they spring from the well of the Spirit and following Christ and the gospel, they eventually subvert the Roman way of life. Again, Christopher Hoklotubbe calls this term a "sly civility" (Hoklotubbe, *Civilized Piety*).

A "good minister" or a "beautiful servant" of the gospel points out what Paul has just exhorted Timothy to teach (that is, 3:14–4:5). If Timothy does this, he will find himself "nourished" on the gospel teaching (again, 3:16). Those who know the glories of that gospel will "have nothing to do with godless myths and old wives' tales" (4:7). Though the Greek term for "old wives' tales" evokes old women, there is a danger of such a translation sliding into sexist language. The NRSV's updated edition thus translates it "profane and foolish tales." Phil Towner gets to the nub of Paul's intent when he says these terms point to "the heresy as pagan in its thrust and insignificant in its contribution" (Towner, *Letters*, 305).

The vision for the right kind of life (*eusebeia*) transcends current life because such people "have put our hope in the living God, who is the Savior of all people, and especially of those who believe" (4:10). Many today diminish the significance of the afterlife and of heaven, but those who do are knocking many verses right out of the New Testament, including this one. Living now in light of God's future for us, the new heaven and new earth, the new Jerusalem, the kingdom of God, heaven—whatever you call it—reveals the wisdom of gospel living (McKnight, *The Heaven Promise*). One more time, then, Paul connects what one believes with one's behavior, tying both strings into a tight knot of unity. How one lives is what one believes, and what one believes shapes how one lives.

BASICS OF MODELING

Evidently, some considered Timothy too young to be instructing those who had some seniority. As in our day, the meaning of calling someone "young" differed from person to person. The following sidebar from the later rabbis could perhaps be a ballpark estimation. Perhaps numbers one through six or seven are for someone who is "young." In the final paragraph of today's passage, Paul, in spite of those charges of Timothy being too young, encourages Timothy by affirming his giftedness, his maturity, and his life as a model for all. Here's how he says it, and Paul's words open up a window on how older leaders can publicly affirm younger leaders in a manner that encourages the younger leaders to carry on:

From the *Mishnah, Avot* 5:21:

(1) At five to Scripture, (2) ten to Mishnah, (3) thirteen to religious duties, (4) fifteen to Talmud, (5) eighteen to the wedding canopy, (6) twenty to responsibility for providing for a

family, (7) thirty to fullness of strength, (8) forty to understanding, (9) fifty to counsel, (10) sixty to old age, (11) seventy to ripe old age, (12) eighty to remarkable strength, (13) ninety to a bowed back, and (14) at a hundred—he is like a corpse who has already passed and gone from this world. (translation Neusner, *The Mishnah*)

First, Paul affirms Timothy's status by saying "Don't let anyone look down on you because you are young" (4:12). Ours is a culture in which youth means relevance and seniority means irrelevance, and that's why many churches are led by . . . well, how to put this not so gently . . . young bucks who have not yet formed mature enough characters for the long haul of church leadership. (Names omitted.)

Second, he affirms Timothy's capacity to be an "example" (4:12), and over time the folks in the church will see how he has advanced in both behavior and belief (4:15). As an example, Timothy was to embody the beliefs and behaviors that witnessed to the gospel. As an example, Timothy could be followed. As an example, Timothy could counter the false teachings running around in the house churches of Ephesus.

Third, Paul advises two practices that can promote the first two points just made: "devote yourself to the public reading of Scripture" and to the exercise of his gifts of "preaching" and "teaching" (4:13–14). In other words, Timothy was gifted by God, and he was called by God, so he was not to neglect that gift. In these two practices Timothy could model the way for the follower of Jesus to live.

Fourth, faithful exercise of one's gifts over time permits others to observe and see one's "progress" (4:15). Timothy's private life could not be seen; it was his public life that was visible, and, over time, Ephesians could narrate a story of how this man Timothy lived.

Could the essential connection of faith and practice, what made up his life as an example, be said any more forcefully than, "Watch your life and doctrine closely" (4:16)? Not just intellectual rigor, not just theological mastery, not just exegesis of the text. No, the leader herself blends *both* intellectual growth and practice to become *eusebeia*, a socially respectable example of the life God wants. If you, leader, do this—get this in hand—"you will save both yourself and your hearers" (4:16).

Master the basics.

QUESTIONS FOR REFLECTION AND APPLICATION

1. What connects the basics on Christian belief and the basics of Christian behavior?

2. How does Paul tie together food, sex, and creation?

3. How does "sly civility" function for the church in the Roman Empire?

4. Have you ever been dismissed because you are "too young" or "too old"? What was that experience like?

5. What are the gifts God has given you to serve the church that you should not neglect?

FOR FURTHER READING

McKnight, Scot. *The Heaven Promise: Engaging the Bible's Truth about Life to Come.* Colorado Springs: WaterBrook, 2015.
Neusner, Jacob. *The Mishnah: A New Translation.* New Haven: Yale, 1991.

LEADERS NURTURE A FAMILY CULTURE

1 Timothy 5:1–2

¹ Do not rebuke an older man harshly, but exhort him as if he were your father. Treat younger men as brothers, ² older women as mothers, and younger women as sisters, with absolute purity.

In fewer than twenty words in Greek, which took thirty-three words for the NIV to translate, Paul instructs Timothy to nurture a family culture in the church. His instructions concern "an older man" and "younger men," and then "older women" and "younger women."

FAMILY RELATIONS

The older men are to be spoken with "as if he were your father." Notice what this means for Paul. Timothy is not to scold, or come down on, or rebuke an older man, but *instead*, his words are to take on a respectful form of communication that fits the word "exhort," or better yet "encourage." The Greek term is *parakaleō*, which as a noun is "Paraclete," which is often translated "advocate." Paul's instruction turns the tone from the negative to the positive. The reason for this is wisdom. Older men and women have a lifetime of experience to offer.

There are three more, less specific, instructions for various groups: the younger men are to be treated as brothers, the older women as mothers, and the younger women as sisters, with an added bit of wisdom that in our world deserves books: "with absolute purity" (5:2). After some observations about a wisdom culture, I will offer observations about "purity" as well.

WISDOM CULTURE

Thomas Bergler, in two important books, maps a history of the American church, concentrating at times from the 1930s to the 1960s on the powerful influence of Youth for Christ, in its move to make the church relevant for the youth they feared they might lose. The result of which, Bergler shows, was the "juvenilization of American Christianity." He does not hold back: instead of a church moving toward wisdom and maturity, an increasing number of church leaders became hip and cool and relevant. Bergler is not foolish, and his book is not composed of finger-pointing. Instead, juvenilization, tied as it was in the 1960s to a shallower, easier-to-believe gospel and a thinner than shallow discipleship demand, led to a generation of satisfied, immature Christians and churches.

> Beginning in the 1930s and 1940s, three factors combined to create the juvenilization of American Christianity. First, new and more powerful youth cultures created distance between adults and adolescents. Second, in an attempt to convert, mobilize, or just hang on to their teenage children, Christian adults adapted the faith to adolescent tastes. As a result of these first two factors,

the stereotypical youth group that combines fun and games with a brief, entertaining religious message was born. In the years since, this model of youth ministry has become a taken-for-granted part of church life. Finally, the journey to adulthood became longer and more confusing, with maturity now just one among many options. The result was juvenilization: the process by which the religious beliefs, practices, and developmental characteristics of adolescents become accepted—or even celebrated—as appropriate for Christians of all ages. (*From Here to Maturity*, 1–2)

The biggest impact of this juvenilization is the widespread absence of a wisdom culture in churches. Age is not the point. Wisdom is. Some old people are old fools, and some younger people are wiser than owls. Relevance and wisdom do not always walk hand in hand; young and wisdom do not always walk hand in hand. Wisdom requires merely giving the sages of your church status and presence in the room where it happens. Wise leaders seek out sages, and they listen to sages with what I have often called "receptive reverence." Their wisdom is not infallible, but only a rash fool ignores what sages have to say (Proverbs 1:2–7).

WITH PURITY

Paul told Timothy to tell the young men—which no doubt would include all men—to relate to, behave with, and to treat the younger women (1) "as sisters" and (2) with "absolute purity." The word "absolute" exaggerates for emphasis: the Greek term is *pas* and means "all" or "every," and along with "absolute" one could translate with "total" or "complete." The term "purity" could be translated as "devotion" with a strong sense of embodied respect.

61

The instruction does not put the responsibility on the woman (1) to take a purity pledge, (2) to wear a purity ring, (3) to change how she dresses, (4) to think of herself as a sex target, (5) or to become the one who fights off the men. Timothy is to tell the young men that their responsibility as Christian men marked by "civilized piety" is to conduct themselves with women in a way that matches how Christ would relate with women. The words that come to mind are to be treated with respect and equality, as fellow disciples, and with embodied honor and verbal dignity. The juvenilization of the church has turned what was supposed to be maturing and mature men into wanting to be endlessly young men driven by hormones.

The concerns here have turned churches into a disgrace where pastor after pastor has abused younger women, where church investigation after investigation has dismissed the allegations, and where women increasingly are no longer safe in the presence of men—in the very place where Paul told Timothy that the younger men (and all men) are to nurture a culture of family relations where respect, dignity, and purity would flourish.

QUESTIONS FOR REFLECTION AND APPLICATION

1. How did a desire to reach young people in American church history lead to the "juvenilization" of the church?

2. What impact did this reduction in maturity have on the church?

3. What happens when a wisdom culture goes missing in a church?

4. How do church abuse cases show a disregard for Paul's instructions to Timothy about purity?

5. Which does you church struggle with more—wisdom or purity? Why?

FOR FURTHER READING

Bergler, Thomas. *From Here to Maturity: Overcoming the Juvenilization of American Christianity.* Grand Rapids: Eerdmans, 2014.
———. *The Juvenilization of American Christianity.* Grand Rapids: Eerdmans, 2012.

McKnight, Scot. "James' Secret: Wisdom in James in the Mode of Receptive Reverence." Pages 201–16 in *Preaching Character: Reclaiming Wisdom's Paradigmatic Imagination for Transformation*. Edited by D. Bland and D. Fleer. Abilene Texas: Abilene University Press, 2010.

LEADERS SEE
WIDOWS

1 Timothy 5:3–16

³ *Give proper recognition to those widows who are really in need.*
⁴ *But if a widow has children or grandchildren, these should learn first of all to put their religion into practice by caring for their own family and so repaying their parents and grandparents, for this is pleasing to God.* ⁵ *The widow who is really in need and left all alone puts her hope in God and continues night and day to pray and to ask God for help.* ⁶ *But the widow who lives for pleasure is dead even while she lives.* ⁷ *Give the people these instructions, so that no one may be open to blame.* ⁸ *Anyone who does not provide for their relatives, and especially for their own household, has denied the faith and is worse than an unbeliever.*

⁹ *No widow may be put on the list of widows unless she is over sixty, has been faithful to her husband,* ¹⁰ *and is well known for her good deeds, such as bringing up children, showing hospitality, washing the feet of the Lord's people, helping those in trouble and devoting herself to all kinds of good deeds.*

¹¹ *As for younger widows, do not put them on such a list. For when their sensual desires overcome their dedication to Christ, they want to marry.* ¹² *Thus they bring judgment on themselves, because they have broken their first pledge.* ¹³ *Besides, they get into the habit*

of being idle and going about from house to house. And not only do they become idlers, but also busybodies who talk nonsense, saying things they ought not to. ¹⁴ So I counsel younger widows to marry, to have children, to manage their homes and to give the enemy no opportunity for slander. ¹⁵ Some have in fact already turned away to follow Satan.

¹⁶ If any woman who is a believer has widows in her care, she should continue to help them and not let the church be burdened with them, so that the church can help those widows who are really in need.

One of the red-letter items on a church's mission is turning invisible people into visible siblings who experience love, integrity, and respect in the household of faith. When I think of who is invisible in our churches, I know the reason they're invisible is mostly various forms of discrimination. So let's think of children, the marginalization of race and ethnic groups, gender bias against women, the poor, the doubters, the urban versus suburban tension, educational attainments, wealth, status, power, and the size of one's home, not to ignore where one has traveled. And what about introverts versus extroverts, knowing that churches tend to be managed by and favor extroverts. Add in those who have experienced abuse in churches. And here's one we have not mentioned but which is the focus of 1 Timothy 5: widows, who map onto a few of the categories of people whom our churches make invisible.

WISDOM FROM A WIDOW

Church policy, shaped by and implemented by leaders, tends to work from the offices into the pews. Which means—and how can one say this gently?—mostly married men, with some married women (at times but not always), decide what kind of ministry a church can have toward widows—that is, if widows even come into consideration.

This is backward. The best thing to do is for the office folks to sit down with widows and let them talk—in safety. The widows know what widows need, and often those in the front offices don't, or at least they need to be educated to form a fuller perspective.

If wisdom means learning to listen to the sages in your midst, no one offers more wisdom on widows than the sage Miriam Neff, who wrote in *Christianity Today* these words:

> I am part of the fastest growing demographic in the United States. We are targeted by new-home builders and surveyed by designers. We are a lucrative niche for health and beauty products, and financial planners invite us to dinners. It's no wonder the marketers are after us: 800,000 join our ranks every year.
>
> Who are we? We are the *invisible* among you—the widows.
>
> Studies show that widows lose 75 percent of their friendship network when they lose a spouse. Sixty percent of us experience serious health issues in that first year. One third of us meet the criteria for clinical depression in the first month after our spouse's death, and half of us remain clinically depressed a year later. Most experience financial decline. One pastor described us by saying we move from the front row of the church to the back, and then out the door. We move from serving and singing in choir to solitude and silent sobbing, and then on to find a place where we belong. (Neff, "The Widow's Might")

I didn't know about how invisible widows are in churches until Kris and I sat down with Miriam after reading her wonderful, every-church-leader-should-own book *From One Widow to Another*. So I have an assignment: start listening today.

WISDOM ABOUT WIDOWS

Widows today are not much different from widows in Paul's day. I want to correct that: the early churches right away not only developed a listening ear to widows, but they also got to work developing ministries for widows and empowered them to develop ministries themselves. One reason why is that the early church was especially sensitive to the poor, and widows were vulnerable and found early church compassion an embodied act of gospel grace. Paul, the sage, gives six bits of wisdom to a budding sage, Timothy, who passes that wisdom on to future sages in the churches of Ephesus. His wisdom emerged from the experiences in his churches of caring for widows, and his experiences will not be the same as ours, but the principle obtains: care for widows.

First, turn the widows from invisible into visible. I'm no fan of the NIV's "give proper recognition" (5:3). Paul chose a dynamic, socially invested term that is best translated "honor." Again, it is a socially respectable faith to give social honor to widows, and on top of that, honoring widows was an integral part of Judaism (Deuteronomy 10:18; 14:29; 16:11, 14; 24:17, 19–21; 26:12–13; 27:19). To make widows visible does not mean one has to ask from the platform, "Would all the widows stand up?" No, honor them as people, with a name, with a story or eight, and not as people with a label to be checked off.

Second, a problem arose in the early churches that some got on the official list of widows (who needed various forms of support) who were not "real widows." That is, they could either care for themselves or they already had adequate support. So Paul wants to make sure the widows on the care-for list are real widows (5:3). Such a widow has no family ("left all alone") and has learned to live by faith (5:5), while some other widows are living for material luxuries, and so they mooch the church for what they can get (5:6). The real widow is put on some register, a care-for list of some kind, because she is marked by the following traits: "(1) over sixty, (2) has been faithful to her husband, (3) and is well known for her good deeds, such as (4) bringing up children, (5) showing hospitality, (6) washing the feet of the Lord's people, (7) helping those in trouble and (8) devoting herself to all kinds of good deeds" (5:9–10, numbers added).

Third, Paul urges children to care for their parents if they are able (5:3) and, to tighten the screw, says the one who doesn't care for their relatives has "denied the faith and is worse than an unbeliever" (5:8). Abandoning a widow, who is the relative in mind here, to be destitute reveals a character without either respect or love.

Fourth, experience revealed that 'younger widows"— again "younger" was flexible—brought out a special kind of treatment, a rather bald one: "don't put them on such a list" (5:11). Not because the churches lack compassion or a socially respectable way of life but because younger widows get remarried, and the resources that could be used for the older widows are used up. There are some sharp edges to what Paul says here, and we have to guess to fill in the empty spaces. A close reading shows that the issues are threefold: (1) age, and thus being remarriageable; (2) sensual desire to be with men (5:11); and (3) violating a pledge, and this pledge is to Christ and the fear is walking away (5:12). With the lines filled in, it appears these younger widows are choosing mates or a way of life that somehow leads them to walk away from the faith.

That's what we can see, even if a little also between the

lines, in what Paul writes in verse 13, which reads "Besides, they get into the habit of being idle and going about from house to house. And not only do they become idlers, but also busybodies who talk nonsense, saying things they ought not to." We can't miss that these women, like the women of 1 Timothy 2, are advised to get married, to have children, to manage their homes, and to avoid giving in to Satan (5:14–15). It appears then that Paul knows that some younger women have been on the list but then subsequently abandoned the faith to enter into a more high-status kind of life.

Before Paul turns to the "elders" in 5:17, he offers wisdom for a believing woman who cares for widows (5:16). This woman is not a family member but instead a financially able woman who has chosen to care for widows. Thank God for those who are generous to widows. Such people make it possible, as was the case with families supporting widows, for the church to be more generous and perhaps also to care for even more widows.

QUESTIONS FOR REFLECTION AND APPLICATION

1. What makes widows invisible in churches?

2. What were the troubles facing widows in Paul's churches?

3. Why does Paul give different advice to older widows and younger widows?

4. Who is invisible in your church? Which groups of people or individuals?

5. What can you do to see them and serve them this week?

FOR FURTHER READING

Neff, Miriam. *From One Widow to Another: Conversations on the New You*. Chicago: Moody, 2009.

———. "The Widow's Might." *Christianity Today*. January 18, 2008. https://www.christianity today.com/ct/2008/january/26.42.html.

LEADERS
NURTURE
ELDERS

1 Timothy 5:17–25

[17] *The elders who direct the affairs of the church well are worthy of double honor, especially those whose work is preaching and teaching.* [18] *For Scripture says, "Do not muzzle an ox while it is treading out the grain," and "The worker deserves his wages."* [19] *Do not entertain an accusation against an elder unless it is brought by two or three witnesses.* [20] *But those elders who are sinning you are to reprove before everyone, so that the others may take warning.* [21] *I charge you, in the sight of God and Christ Jesus and the elect angels, to keep these instructions without partiality, and to do nothing out of favoritism.*

[22] *Do not be hasty in the laying on of hands, and do not share in the sins of others. Keep yourself pure.*

[23] *Stop drinking only water, and use a little wine because of your stomach and your frequent illnesses.*

[24] *The sins of some are obvious, reaching the place of judgment ahead of them; the sins of others trail behind them.* [25] *In the same way, good deeds are obvious, and even those that are not obvious cannot remain hidden forever.*

In the first verse of chapter 5, Paul wrote about elders but most translations make it clear that the term there refers to an older man. In today's passage the identical term is used. Again, most translations do something similar: the older man here is a leader in the church whom we have always called an elder or, if one is in some denominations, a "presbyter." (Presbyter transliterates the Greek word.) Both passages refer to a senior, an older man (see numbers 8–14 in the *Mishnah, Avot* quote, pp. 55–56). A maturing with age—that is, wisdom or sagacity—mattered most. Our passage instructs Timothy how to treat the Christian sages of the community.

PAY THE LEADERS WHO TEACH

"Elders" engage the community of faith in two ways. First, they "direct the affairs of the church" (5:17), and here the NIV has gone above and beyond the words. The Greek only has the verb that means "leading," and the term means "stand in front" or "stand ahead," and that's it. Here's a more literal translation: "The leading-well elders" (5:17). Second, either some or all of these leading-well elders lead in "preaching and teaching," and here again the NIV adds to the text. The text does not use "preaching" but, again literally, reads "the ones laboring in word and teaching." "Word" and "teaching" refer to the same gift being exercised.

We should not think of someone standing behind a pulpit but of someone in a circle of other believers, informing and instructing them. Leading-well elders who instruct the believers are worthy of a "double honor." The meaning of "double honor" is not entirely clear but most likely means respect and remuneration (Fee, *1 and 2 Timothy, Titus*, 129). Either that or Paul means they deserve our honor. But because Paul goes on in verse 18 to evoke material provision in two quotations—one from the Old Testament (Deuteronomy 25:4) and one from Jesus (Luke 10:7), the word "double" is best understood as respect and remuneration. Those who guide churches through instruction are honored by the church providing funds for them so they can devote their energies to teaching, which requires time and tranquility (cf. Acts 6:1–7). Raising the question of a leader's salary or pay can provoke controversy, but when I'm asked, I put it this way: the wisest approaches pay the pastor the average salary of those who attend the church. I was told that by a sage years back.

PROTECT LEADERS AND REBUKE LEADERS

Paul wants Timothy to nurture a culture that not only honors the elders but also respects them enough to protect them and also respects truth enough to rebuke them when they have sinned (5:19–20). Protecting means not permitting false and trivial accusations against elders, so Paul appeals to the Jewish "two or three witnesses" tradition (Deuteronomy 19:15). The two-or-three-witness principle has limits and cannot be used in all cases. Some pastors violate their marriage, their sacred calling, and the integrity of a victim, *and in almost 100 percent of the cases do so in private*, which means there is neither a second nor a third witness. If one required this in all cases, one would nurture a culture of power and sexual abuse.

Give Deuteronomy 22:23–24 a careful reading first. Here the violation occurs in a context when a woman could have screamed for help but didn't. Both are considered guilty. In 22:25–27 the situation changes: the two are "out in the country," and the man is considered guilty because it is assumed not only that the woman would have screamed for help against her rapist but also that her word is trustworthy—and there are no witnesses. This is the same book of Moses that instituted the two-or-three-witness tradition. If there are perfectly reasonable exceptions there, there are also exceptions to 1 Timothy 5:19. In the last three years, I have heard, including in our own church, as many as two hundred stories about power and sexual abuse in institutions. In almost all of them, multiple stories spill out onto one another toward power abuse, while the stories about sexual abuse, always one-on-one situations, come forward privately and secretively and only later into the light. In many of the sexual abuse cases, once one or two people broke open the stories, others came forward. These are the sorts of two-or-three-witness situations that will most often emerge in churches. But at times it's one person with one other person in private, and in those situations the church needs to be wise and transparent as it seeks the truth. The percentage of allegations that are false is very low.

Backing up now: Paul urges Timothy, as the NIV has it, "to reprove before everyone" (5:20) the sinning elders (who then are not leading-well elders). "Reprove" or "rebuke" are fair translations, but there is a sense of convincing and even persuading the household of faith of the sinful action of the elder. The angle Paul has on this is that the public convincing will create the fear of God in people.

DON'T BE PARTIAL TOWARD LEADERS

We want to trust our church leaders, and I'm glad we do. But we want also to do the right thing and bring light into the darkness. Walking that balance requires sages in the room, which is why Paul urges Timothy to find leaders who will put all partiality behind when dealing with accusations. So important is this principle of transparent impartiality that Paul intensifies his words with "I charge you, in the sight of God and Christ Jesus and the elect angels . . ." (5:21). He uses two words for bias: "without partiality" and "nothing out of favoritism." The images used evoke prejudging (prejudice) and leaning toward—all in advance of the discovery and presentation of the evidence.

From my experience over the last few years, since the Willow Creek story broke and I wrote a book with my daughter, Laura Barringer, *A Church Called Tov*, and a forthcoming second book called *Pivot*, I would say most people believe the pastor and most people don't believe those bringing allegations. Any prejudice or leaning toward, then, needs to be resisted with intentional acts toward transparency and honesty.

PLACE HANDS ON LEADERS AFTER FULL CONSIDERATION

Because at times the sins of leaders will have to be exposed to the assembly, Paul urges Timothy not to be "hasty in the laying on of hands" because, in so doing, he will become complicit in the sins of fellow leaders. So he ends this brief protocol with "keep yourself pure," which suggests both Timothy avoiding such sins and not becoming complicit in sin-soaked elders by carelessly approving eldership (5:22).

If only there were a fool-proof process of interviewing and selecting leaders! There is not one, and any church with a history knows some mistaken appointments have occurred. But some of these steps could help (and perhaps you have others): Ensure there is at least one wise, perceptive psychologist in the interview process. (I always say, not whimsically, for every lawyer or executive businessman on a committee, you need two psychologists.) Select people of character for your search committee. Minimize the number of alpha males in the interviews. Ensure an equal representation of men and women in the process, as well as that the group reflects the demographics of your church. Require the prospective leader be given a full psychological test that can be analyzed by a psychologist who can be given veto power (and thus not have to disclose what should not be disclosed). Acquire good evaluations of the person from previous employers, which means not relying solely on references the prospective leader provides. Avoid perceiving the future leader as a platformed preacher, and instead envision her as a sage, as a follower of Jesus, and as a person with clear, Christian character. Consider the age of the prospective leader, and balance the ages of those on the search committee. (And compare the person with Mr. Rogers. You will rise up and call me "Blessed" if you do that.)

OTHER STUFF

Sometimes Paul gets personal and quotidian about what he writes. We get some of that now. Timothy evidently has stomach issues, perhaps irritable bowel syndrome, so Paul recommends avoiding water and drinking some wine (5:23). Water then was not purified, so all sorts of problems arose from drinking ordinary water from rivers and cisterns.

Paul knows that character eventually reveals itself (5:24–25). The "sins of some are [as] obvious" as the "good deeds" of others. He knows from experience that eventually a person's true character and behaviors will come to the surface. Because the search process rarely permits a decade of observing someone, what Paul says here takes us right back to what he said about leading-well elders and sinning elders. Be careful, but know that at times mistakes will be made.

QUESTIONS FOR REFLECTION AND APPLICATION

1. What are some traits of a leading-well elder?

2. How can church teams both protect and rebuke leaders?

3. In what ways can we apply Paul's advice for selecting elders to today's proliferation of church abuse scandals?

4. How can selection or search teams avoid partiality today?

5. How much do you think a pastor should be paid? What factors do you take into consideration for that calculation?

FOR FURTHER READING

McKnight, Scot, and Laura Barringer. *A Church Called Tov: Forming a Goodness Culture that Resists Abuses of Power and Promotes Healing*. Carol Stream, IL: Tyndale Momentum, 2020.

LEADERS RECOGNIZE TIME-BOUND INSTRUCTIONS

1 Timothy 6:1–2

[1] All who are under the yoke of slavery should consider their masters worthy of full respect, so that God's name and our teaching may not be slandered. [2] Those who have believing masters should not show them disrespect just because they are fellow believers. Instead, they should serve them even better because their masters are dear to them as fellow believers and are devoted to the welfare of their slaves.

These are the things you are to teach and insist on.

The most important words Paul uses here are "slavery" and "slaves." Keith Bradley, one of the world's experts on Roman slavery, defines a slave as it should be defined: "Slavery by definition is a means of securing and maintaining an involuntary labour force by a group in society which monopolises political and economic power" (Bradley, *Slaves and Masters*, 18).

Slavery in the Roman world was about status and integrity and identity, all three reshaped by turning a person into a utility. Most slaves were born into slavery, and a slave's life was dependent on the master's character. A male slave remained in the status of a "boy" his entire life, unless emancipated, to prevent a legal marriage, legal control of (their nonlegal marital relationship) children, and thus legal inheritance rights. Slaves were commonly abused physically and sexually, and many female slaves were sex slaves to their masters. (I will use another version of this paragraph in my comments about Philemon, p. 208.)

I want to make two observations, and they will not be comfortable for some. First it is a very, very serious mistake to pretend that slavery then was not the same as slavery in the New World. It's a similar mistake to think of Roman slavery along the lines of modern employment. A slave is an owned body. Furthermore, the word "slave" is a label that devalues a person's dignity, agency, and social status. It is better to say "enslaved person" than "slave," but the harshness of the first century was simply not enlightened. Which brings our next point.

Second, Paul and Timothy did not perceive the immorality and hideousness of slavery. They swam in waters boiling with slavery and did not perceive they were boiling themselves. There is nothing about this slavery text that easily transfers into our world. Yes, it was beneficial for those who lived in a world of slavery to work in a way that did not get the gospel mission into any more trouble than it was already in. Yes, it is good for people to work for their bosses as people who are serving God and not their bosses, but this text is not about pragmaticism, workers, and bosses but about masters and slaves. It belongs in that world, and I shall leave it there.

THESE MATTERS

One of my sharp-eyed editors once told me that I use too many pronominals, and what he said of me, he'd say of

Paul's "these" in verse 2. Does "These" refer to the previous teachings or to what follows? He could have said "These instructions in 5:1–6:2" or "These principles I'm about to write about in 6:3–10." He didn't tell us explicitly, so we have to decide to what "these" refers. The NIV and the NRSVue have decided Paul's "these" was forward pointing—that is, he was pointing us all toward 6:3–10—while the Common English Bible places it as I have—at the end of verse 2 with a hard break at 6:3.

The language of Paul, literally, is "These teach and encourage." These matters pertain to the whole of 5:1–6:2, as he wants Timothy to press upon the Ephesians what a socially respectable Christian way of life looks like.

QUESTIONS FOR REFLECTION AND APPLICATION

1. How does slavery turn a person into a utility?

2. What mistakes can readers make when reading biblical texts about slavery?

3. What is the value of leaving texts like this about slavery in the world where they belong, rather than trying to import them into our world?

4. How have you heard biblical slavery passages taught in the past?

5. What impact does this study have on your understanding of interpreting biblical words on slavery?

FOR FURTHER READING

Bradley, Keith R. *Slaves and Masters in the Roman Empire: A Study in Social Control.* New York: Oxford University Press, 1987.

LEADERS LIVE
PRINCIPLED LIVES

1 Timothy 6:3–10

[3] *If anyone teaches otherwise and does not agree to the sound instruction of our Lord Jesus Christ and to godly teaching,* [4] *they are conceited and understand nothing. They have an unhealthy interest in controversies and quarrels about words that result in envy, strife, malicious talk, evil suspicions* [5] *and constant friction between people of corrupt mind, who have been robbed of the truth and who think that godliness is a means to financial gain.*

[6] *But godliness with contentment is great gain.* [7] *For we brought nothing into the world, and we can take nothing out of it.* [8] *But if we have food and clothing, we will be content with that.* [9] *Those who want to get rich fall into temptation and a trap and into many foolish and harmful desires that plunge people into ruin and destruction.* [10] *For the love of money is a root of all kinds of evil. Some people, eager for money, have wandered from the faith and pierced themselves with many griefs.*

Principles provide guiding lights. An influential person in your church, say, goes off to a special conference and comes back with a never-heard-of-before idea. The person is so excited about it, she starts telling everyone about it, and before long one small group after another is reading that conference speaker's book. The problem is, the speaker's got a good idea presented as the most important idea ever. When a minor idea gets major, the major ideas become minor, and the next thing you know, we've got one person arguing with another. When I was teaching at a college, a student of ours went off to a conference that pushed the ideas of Calvinism really hard. The student came back totally persuaded, and before long he was arguing with me, my colleagues, and others in our class. It seemed he was arguing with people everywhere he went. Paul weighs in with a principle.

THE LIVED THEOLOGY PRINCIPLE

I translate: "If someone teaches other teachings and doesn't approach the healthy words of our Lord Jesus Christ, and with teaching consistent with civilized piety" (6:3, The Second Testament). One of Paul's principles, which can be called the gospel principle, combines two elements: teach the gospel about Jesus Christ and live in a way that is consistent with the gospel. Believing the right things about Jesus's life and what Jesus said, what he did, how he died, was buried, and rose again—that's not enough. One's beliefs need to be reflected consistently in one's life. The gospel principle can be called *lived theology*. Lived theology is a life that tells the gospel by the way one lives. In the Pastoral Letters of Paul, lived theology is often called *eusebeia*, or "civilized piety."

Paul learned from experience in his churches that what they taught mattered but what they taught could be degraded and discredited by the way they lived. Here, nearer the end of his life, he's pushing very hard the principle of lived theology.

Flipping the script, Paul discredits those whose theology is an unlived theology or, perhaps better, a contradictory life. Think today of the number of pastors—some well-known—whose lives discredited the gospel by how their sexual power-abusing behaviors contradicted the faith they preached from the platform. The concern with the leaders' way of life shaped everything Paul said about character in 1 Timothy 3:1–12. So Paul says such people are "conceited" and "understand nothing" (6:4) and people who are divisive and who have "robbed of the truth." His last few words of 6:5, which I translate as "thinking civilized piety is cash," leads him to his second principle.

THE CONTENTMENT PRINCIPLE

A good lived theology, because it is consistent, witnesses to the gospel not only by a consistency but also by *material and financial contentment*. Paul's hands grip funds loosely. One way of expressing this principle is "We brought nothing into the world, and we can take nothing out of it" (6:7). Undergirding this principle is that life now will end and then eternity. A consistent-with-the-gospel lived theology lives now in light of eternity. What is more, Paul knows that the final kingdom of God has reached from the future back into the present time and draws us to live now "as if"—that is, as if the kingdom were now. What matters is that the final kingdom will not be marked by inequality or inequity. All will be like the children of Israel collecting manna for each day: enough for that day and no more.

The desire for riches, for luxury, for status, for one's possessions and house and clothing and cars and vacations—leads such people "into temptation and a trap" because they are driven by "many foolish and harmful desires that plunge people into ruin and destruction" (6:9). He lays down a second expression of the contentment principle: "For the love of money is a root of all kinds of evil" (6:10). The terms Paul uses are picturesque: "silver-love" (love of money) and "craving" (eager for money). Paul knows these people no better than you and I know such people, and we may also know the collapse of such persons.

Principles guide us, and few principles can guide more of our lives than the lived theology principle and the contentment principle. Kris and I recently watched with our son's family (Lukas, Annika, Aksel, and Finley) the wonderful movie about the great basketball player for the Milwaukee Bucks, Giannis Sina Ugo Antetokounmpo, called *Rise*. In a climactic scene, complicated by a family in financial free fall, Giannis's star was rising, a good-hearted agent was working a deal for him to get the kind of playing opportunity to do well financially, when another, but slimy, agent drops by, hands over a few thousand euros, and promises a different contract. The family gets together and, on the basis of the Christian principles of "true to one's word" and 'contentment," shews away the slimy agent—and the rest is history. Giannis led his team to the NBA championship, and he is a certain future Hall of Famer. But the family's lived theology tells even more than Giannis's hoop capacities. His born name, misspelled in Greece on official documents, is "Adetokunbo" (The Crown Has Returned from Overseas). Indeed.

QUESTIONS FOR REFLECTION AND APPLICATION

1. What is the lived theology principle?

2. What connects civilized piety with lived theology?

3. How does a good lived theology lead to contentment?

4. What are some ways you live out your beliefs?

5. How content are you with your financial or material situation? What might Paul's advice say to you?

A LEADER'S
TEN VIRTUES

1 Timothy 6:11–21

[11] *But you, man of God, (1*) flee from all this, and pursue (2) righteousness, (3) godliness, (4) faith, (5) love, (6) endurance and (7) gentleness.* [12] *(8) Fight the good fight of the faith. (9) Take hold of the eternal life to which you were called when you made your good confession in the presence of many witnesses.* [13] *In the sight of God, who gives life to everything, and of Christ Jesus, who while testifying before Pontius Pilate made the good confession, I charge you* [14] *(10) to keep this command without spot or blame until the appearing of our Lord Jesus Christ,* [15] *which God will bring about in his own time—God, the blessed and only Ruler, the King of kings and Lord of lords,* [16] *who alone is immortal and who lives in unapproachable light, whom no one has seen or can see. To him be honor and might forever. Amen.*

[17] *Command those who are rich in this present world not to be arrogant nor to put their hope in wealth, which is so uncertain, but to put their hope in God, who richly provides us with everything for our enjoyment.* [18] *Command them to do good, to be rich in good deeds, and to be generous and willing to share.* [19] *In this way they will lay up treasure for themselves as a firm foundation for the coming age, so that they may take hold of the life that is truly life.*

20 Timothy, guard what has been entrusted to your care. Turn away from godless chatter and the opposing ideas of what is falsely called knowledge, 21 which some have professed and in so doing have departed from the faith.

Grace be with you all.

*Numbers in parentheses added in this passage for ease of reference with what follows.

You may have observed that over and over in this letter, Paul writes directly to Timothy about his own life and not just what Timothy, who is called to form other leaders, is to teach others. The last passage in this letter turns to Timothy, who stands in for the leader who needs to attend to his or her own life even more than to the life of the leaders being formed. What Paul says for Timothy, Timothy knows pertains to all those who are called to various forms of Christian leadership.

In closing the curtains of this personal letter, Paul provides ten virtues of a leader. As I have said in other contexts, let's not make these the most important ten, for Paul doesn't say that. These are virtues of a leader with a character that witnesses to civilized piety or a socially respectable faith.

TEN VIRTUES OF A LEADER

Timothy's sage, Paul, (1) tells him to "flee from all this" (6:11). If we didn't have verse divisions, paragraph divisions, and breaks that form new sections in some Bibles, the "this" from which leaders are to flee would be as clear as a mountain stream. The "this" is the craving for money—that is, greed (6:6–10). So 6:11 is a personal application of what was just taught. The negative (flee from) finds a positive. Instead of greed, he tells Timothy to chase after (2) doing what is right, and once he's got the word chase or "pursue" in setting forth the course of lived theology for Timothy, he adds more terms to what leaders are to be chasing after. The NIV's "godliness," as you know, we have translated as (3) "civilized piety," calling attention once again to the importance of the public face of the Christian leader.

It seems advisable to collect the next four virtues together: (4) faith, (5) love, (6) endurance, and (7) gentleness. Faith always requires the reader to ponder if it means the initial act of trusting, to ongoing trusting (allegiance), or to what one believes (the faith). For Timothy, the second is uppermost in Paul's mind. Faith and love are combined often in the New Testament, sometimes with hope. Love is the supreme Christian virtue in many passages in the New Testament (Mark 12:28–34; 1 Corinthians 13; Galatians 5:21; Romans 13:9–10; 1 John), where it describes a person's commitment and affection for another person, being the person's advocate, and growing together in Christlikeness. That "endurance" appears does not surprise because in this letter hanging on to the faith and to a lived theology consistent with the faith become vitally important. "Gentleness" may well surprise some readers because leadership and gentleness tend to repel one another. But the Christian sense of leadership is marked by love and compassion and grace and service. The word behind "gentleness" occurs exactly one time in the entire New Testament and is yet another of Paul's graphic terms: it evokes a kind of patience or slowness with one's passions, feelings, and emotions. It refers to moderating, subduing, and controlling one's feelings so they don't burst forth in destructive ways.

The next three virtues get more than single-word mentions. (8) "Fight the good fight" (6:12) indicates there are bad fights and there are ways to fight that are good. The good, or beautiful or excellent, fight concerns either the faith itself or a life of allegiance to Christ. Both are true, but I suspect the former is truer! Along with resilience in the battle for a gospel-shaped lived theology, next comes (9) "Take hold of the eternal life" (6:12), which prompts Paul to expand his thoughts (6:12b–13), and some of it provides a rare glimpse into the earlier life of Timothy. The "good confession" (6:13) may point only to the general profession all believers make (e.g., Romans 10:9–10), or it may point back to Timothy's personal confession. Others suggest Paul is thinking back to Timothy's baptism and initial public confession. It must be noted that this "good confession" language is not typical of the New Testament. We find it noticeably about Jesus, who confessed publicly before Pontius Pilate (6:13; cf. Mark 15:1–15), so I think it wise to see here a general confession (e.g., Romans 10:9–10).

Grabbing hold of a confession of eternal life unfolds into his tenth virtue: "Keep this command" (6:14). Just what the "command" is Paul does not say explicitly, but it seems he's got that "good confession" in mind. Paul's attention is not fixed on the content of the command but the length of time. He wants Timothy to remain faithful—that is, "without spot or blame" (6:14)—and that faithfulness has a timestamp on it: "until the appearing [same word as epiphany] of our Lord Jesus Christ" (6:14), which will happen in God's good time. To make it very clear, God gets some definition here: "God, the blessed and only Ruler, the King of kings and Lord of lords, who alone is immortal and who lives in unapproachable light, whom no one has seen or can see." To each of the twenty-one times God is explicitly mentioned in 1 Timothy, this definition could be added.

A FEW MORE INSTRUCTIONS

On top of these ten virtues, Paul reminds Timothy to warn yet again the wealthy in Ephesus not to devote themselves to a greedy way of life (6:17–19). The archaeological site of Ephesus, which is one of the world's great sites, has a main street running downhill toward the ancient port, and at the bottom of the street, to the south side are multistoried homes of the rich and wealthy of Ephesus. The homes, called the "Terrace Houses" (see the For Further Reading section for a link), are not far from the agora, the massive theater, and the port, and one could not have written what Paul wrote and not be thinking of that kind of wealth. Paul urges Timothy to remind the wealthy to put their hope in God, not in wealth; that God will provide; that they are to be generous with their wealth (that's what "to do good" [6:18] means); and that generosity for others provides treasures with God.

One more reminder for Timothy: "guard what has been entrusted to your care" (6:20). "Guard" has three senses: First, to preserve the gospel with clarity and consistency. Second, to live out the gospel in a socially respectable manner of life. The third sense is to stay away from the nonsensical combativeness of teachers who want to embroil others in controversies (cf. again 6:4–5). Divisiveness occurs when the gospel itself gets lost in corrupting barnacles.

A brief prayer works for Timothy, for his churches, and for you and me: "Grace be with you all" (6:21).

QUESTIONS FOR REFLECTION AND APPLICATION

1. What do you find significant in Paul's shift in this section from general advice for Timothy to use in leading the church to personal advice for Timothy's own life?

2. Does "gentleness" as a leadership trait surprise you? Why or why not?

3. Why are social respectability, wealth, and false teaching such important and repeated emphases in this letter?

4. As we conclude 1 Timothy, what stands out to you most about this letter?

5. How do you want to adjust your discipleship life as a result of studying 1 Timothy?

FOR FURTHER READING

Link to Terrace Houses frescos: https://commons
.wikimedia.org/wiki/Category:Frescos_in_the
_Terrace_Houses_(Ephesus)

2 TIMOTHY

LEADERS ARE GOD-DEPENDENT

2 Timothy 1:1–5

¹ Paul, an apostle of Christ Jesus by the will of God, in keeping with the promise of life that is in Christ Jesus,

² To Timothy, my dear son:

Grace, mercy and peace from God the Father and Christ Jesus our Lord.

³ I thank God, whom I serve, as my ancestors did, with a clear conscience, as night and day I constantly remember you in my prayers. ⁴ Recalling your tears, I long to see you, so that I may be filled with joy. ⁵ I am reminded of your sincere faith, which first lived in your grandmother Lois and in your mother Eunice and, I am persuaded, now lives in you also.

Some fashionable book titles begin with "Everything I Ever Needed to Know About . . ." I just looked up some of the completions of those titles: *Everything I've Ever Learned from Things Going Wrong* and *Everything I Ever Needed to Know about Life . . . I Learned in Prison*, and, if I recall it accurately, the original one was *All I Really Need to Know I Learned in Kindergarten* (by Robert Fulghum). The apostle Paul and his close circle of mission agents surely could have written the first two, and though there was no such thing as European kindergartens (a German word, by the way), what he learned about his faith from his parents matches what he says to Timothy about learning the faith from his mother and grandmother.

Paul in this passage makes it clear that what leaders need to know comes from God, so a kind of "Everything I Ever Needed to Know about Leading I Learned from God." It's quite the claim. The claim is not arrogant, but rather it is profoundly humble. Paul, the sage, opens this new letter to the one he has mentored, Timothy, by essentially saying, "What I'm about to write to you owes its origins in God's goodness and grace." As long as one utters such a word from humility and avoids using the terms to clobber someone, like, "It's by God's grace that I tell you that your preaching sucks," the claim anchors ministry in the truth of the gospel instead of in personal charisma or clever leadership skills.

The tendency toward clever leadership skills is a problem these days. Far too many pastors are more in tune with the leadership ideas from business books than they are from the pastoral theology of people who pastor, like Paul and Timothy, like Phoebe and Priscilla, like Barbara Brown Taylor and Lesslie Newbigin. Leaning too much into business leadership manuals creates a business culture in a church instead of a Christlikeness culture and, as the rector of our church told me recently, it turns pastors into CEOs instead of pastors. She added, "Business is also about growth over caring for people. So people who get in the way of growth are seen as obstacles." The business model also concentrates on "branding" and forming "franchises" and turns congregants into "giving units" or "consumers," and then the church leaders are "quantifying" everyone's "production measurements" so one can measure a person for "success" based on "numbers, which never lie." When "success" is measured by "numerical growth," we have abandoned what the gospel says flourishing is. Enough said, let's get to what Paul told Timothy.

GOD'S CALLING

Paul opens this letter by informing Timothy (all over again and again) that his calling as an "apostle of Jesus Christ" occurred only "by the will of God" (1:1). God has a "will," a design and plan for Paul. Paul did not choose this, and he clearly didn't grow up planning on becoming an agent of Jesus Christ to gentiles in the Roman Empire! God ripped apart Paul's life, grabbed his attention on the road to Damascus, and stunned him so much he took note—and turned from an opponent of Jesus to his greatest first-century witness. He could not look back on his life without muttering over and over, "God did it all." Leaders listen carefully to the "by the will of God" phrase, because one's calling is not just a one-and-done thing. As Barbara Brown Taylor observed after decades of pastoring, "If my own experience can be trusted, then God does not call us once but many times. There are calls to faith and calls to ordination, but in between there are calls to particular communities and calls to particular tasks within them—calls into and out of relationships as well as calls to seek God wherever God may be found" (Taylor, *The Preaching Life*, 25).

GOD'S LIFE

God's calling in Paul's life is "in keeping with" or corresponds tightly to the "promise of life that is in Christ Jesus" (1:1). That life is the resurrection; it is eternal life that begins now and explodes into a transformation of our current bodies into bodies fit for the final kingdom of God. A calling consistent with that kind of life never diminishes life now, which in 1 Timothy showed up often as "civilized piety" or "godliness" and shows up again in 2 Timothy 3:5 and Titus 1:1, but instead encompasses both life now and life then.

To intensify this God-dependency, Paul now greets Timothy by once again sketching the most significant resource for leadership: "Grace, mercy and peace" he wishes on Timothy. But they are not his own. Instead, they are "from God the Father and Christ Jesus our Lord" (1:2). Now notice how God-dependent the major terms are: apostle, will, life, grace, mercy, and peace! Christian leaders are reeducated into a new kind of leadership when they realize how God-dependent they are. Their greatest resources are prayer, Bible reading, listening and discerning through the Spirit what God is calling them to do, listening to Spirit-shaped mentors and Spirit-prompted siblings in Christ, and attending to Spirit-led writers.

GOD'S NETWORK

Paul is in prison in Rome. Timothy seems to be in Ephesus. They're best friends who have shared more than twenty years of ministry together. Every time Paul prays, he prays for Timothy. And when he prays for Timothy, he remembers him, and in remembering him, he thanks God "with a clear conscience" (1:3) that reveals a network of God's work in history. Lesslie Newbigin once gave a series of talks to pastors and leaders in India. One of his talks was called "Remembering" and was given to the Armenian Church in Madras. Here was his thesis: "Our faith is a remembering faith; we remember what the Lord has done, and it is through remembering that we come to know him in the present" (Newbigin, *Good Shepherd*, 127).

Notice what happens here: "as my ancestors did" (1:3) indicates Paul's own personal story and his God-dependent, networked connection to the story of Israel going back to Abraham (and Adam and Eve). Paul discovered Timothy in his hometown (Acts 16:1–5), welcomed him onto the team, and learned then and there that Timothy had been discipled into Christ through the faith of his mom and grandmother (2 Timothy 1:5).

Leaders would do well to map their story into a network of relationships that can have only clear origin: in the work of God in this world. My mother was named Lois because of this passage. My father was at first nurtured into faith by his Holiness Pentecostal mom and dad, and then his faith took on a new shape when I was a youngster. Kris's faith was nurtured in her church but took on a new shape itself as did mine when we were at a church camp in high school. And we have faith because of the Baptists and Presbyterians, who go back in bumpy ways to the Reformation and behind that to the early churches and, yes, to Paul and to Jesus—and behind them all the way back to Abraham.

QUESTIONS FOR REFLECTION AND APPLICATION

1. From what authority source does Paul present his wisdom to Timothy?

2. What impact does a business leadership culture have on pastors?

3. How does calling work for a pastor?

4. Through what network did you come to faith?

5. How are you God-dependent in your life?

FOR FURTHER READING

Taylor, Barbara Brown. *The Preaching Life.* Cambridge, MA: Cowley, 1993.

Newbigin, Lesslie. *"The Good Shepherd": Meditations on Christian Ministry in Today's World.* Grand Rapids: Eerdmans, 1977.

LEADERS NURTURE GOD'S GIFTING

2 Timothy 1:6–14

[6] For this reason I remind you to fan into flame the gift of God, which is in you through the laying on of my hands. [7] For the Spirit God gave us does not make us timid, but gives us power, love and self-discipline. [8] So do not be ashamed of the testimony about our Lord or of me his prisoner. Rather, join with me in suffering for the gospel, by the power of God. [9] He has saved us and called us to a holy life—not because of anything we have done but because of his own purpose and grace. This grace was given us in Christ Jesus before the beginning of time, [10] but it has now been revealed through the appearing of our Savior, Christ Jesus, who has destroyed death and has brought life and immortality to light through the gospel. [11] And of this gospel I was appointed a herald and an apostle and a teacher. [12] That is why I am suffering as I am. Yet this is no cause for shame, because I know whom I have believed, and am convinced that he is able to guard what I have entrusted to him until that day.

[13] What you heard from me, keep as the pattern of sound teaching, with faith and love in Christ Jesus. [14] Guard the good deposit that was entrusted to you—guard it with the help of the Holy Spirit who lives in us.

What we are best at in our gifting often comes most naturally, but that gift can be nurtured even more. Those born to teach or mentor or listen or organize can enhance their gifts by observing those more mature in that gift, by educating, by reading, by attending conferences, and by listening and learning from those who can mentor us. Paul was Timothy's mentor, and Paul exhorts Timothy in today's passage to "fan into flame the gift of God" (1:6). Because of the correlation of gifting and natural abilities, we may have a tendency to ignore the origin of the gift (God's Spirit), the challenges gifting includes (suffering), and the importance of our gift being formed in the direction of preserving "sound teaching" (1:13).

GOD'S GIFT THROUGH THE CHURCH

We nurture our gifts when we comprehend their origin in God. I wrote in the previous paragraph about "those born to . . . ," and most of us use that expression or have heard it. There's truth in it, but there's another side to that truth. Timothy's gift, which is not named but at least involves pastoring, leading, teaching, and mentoring others, is the *charisma* from God (or "of" God). Our place, your place, and my place in the family of God is not our decision, not the result of our ambition, and not simply the recognition of our natural abilities. *God* decides where to use us in God's mission in this world. I know of pastors who were theater majors, and they can perform on the stage. Such people can wow their way onto the platform and into the office of pastor. But pastoring transcends performance, and when it doesn't, it is not a gift from God but the result of an actor's ambition. You may be old enough to recall a boy, spiritually abused by his parents by their turning him into a four-year-old preacher, who by his teenage years turned from the faith and became an actor named Marjoe Gortner (*Marjoe*). I use an extreme example, but lesser-known ones, and no less true and sad, are easily found.

God has chosen to distribute gifts through the Spirit but also, in a different way, through hands. Notice what Paul says here: "the gift of God, which is in you through the laying on of *my* hands" (1:6, emphasis added). From God the Father, through the Spirit, but also through the hands of Paul that gift was given to Timothy. Perhaps you get a bit nervous thinking of a human-mediated gift. Gifting through human laying on of hands is as "old" as the Old Testament (Numbers 27:18–23) and as "new" as the New Testament, and it is as "old" as the early church (Acts 8:17–18; 9:12, 17; 19:6) and as "new" as current church practice. My bishop, Todd Hunter, laid his hands on me when I was ordained as a deacon.

But notice that in 1 Timothy, Paul said that gift was distributed to Timothy "through prophecy when the body of elders laid their hands on you" (1 Timothy 4:14). So it was not Paul alone but the leaders of the church who laid hands on him. Paul was one of them. Here then is the actual order of God's distribution of gifts to the church: God the Father, through the Spirit, and often with the laying on of hands by recognized leaders in the church. It is *the Spirit* who "gives us power, love and self-discipline" to exercise the gifts distributed (1:7).

"All is grace" Brennan Manning said of himself when he wrote his autobiography (Manning, *All Is Grace*). God's grace was his surviving companion with his own constant struggles. In the midst of those struggles, Manning exercised his gift of testifying to God's love for sinners regardless. Paul himself cannot speak of gifts (*charismata*) without making it clear it is all grace (*charis*), where he contrasts "his own purpose and grace" with works (NIV translates "works" with something "we have done"' 1:9–10). In this passage "works" will refer either to the works of the law of Moses or to public acts of service for the community. Either way, the concern is a person claiming status on the basis either of law observance or public benevolence. Neither claim works with God. Salvation itself is God's grace toward us, which undergirds our gifts as grace-acts, grace-empowerments, and grace-exercises in the power of God's Spirit.

To nurture our gifts, let us all reflect on their origins and empowering sources: Father, Spirit, mentors, you and me.

GOD'S GIFT IN SUFFERING

Church people, and especially church leaders, can be among the most idealistic and optimistic and unrealistic visionaries. "On innumerable occasions," Dietrich Bonhoeffer wrote in the heat of Nazi Germany's opposition to his underground seminary, "a whole Christian community has been shattered because it has lived on the basis of a wishful image" (Bonhoeffer, *Life Together*, 35). Recently Kris and I visited the Shaker Village of Pleasant Hill in Kentucky. The Shakers not only reacted against the rise of modernity (like the Amish), but they also were driven by a vision that they had entered the millennium, they eschewed all sexual relations, they lived together in communities (like Pleasant Hill), and they only survived by conversions, by welcoming those who wanted to join the community, and by adopting children. There are, according to our tour guide, only two or three Shakers left in the whole world. Their idealism did not and still does not match the reality of God's plan in this world.

A plan that includes suffering. Paul tells Timothy not to be ashamed to stand up for Jesus in this world and to "join with me in suffering for the gospel" and to do so "by the power of God" (1:8). The gift of God to Paul meant he was "a herald and an apostle and a teacher" (1:11), and for the exercising of that gift he was suffering. But he knew personally the One in whom he trusted, and he knew God's empowering grace would sustain him (1:12). We nurture our gifts, once again, by knowing that God is at work in us to empower us to put those gifts into play in God's way in God's place. Because Jesus "destroyed death and has brought life and immortality to light" (1:1), Paul urges Timothy to recognize that exercising God's calling can coexist with suffering and can actually flourish in the midst of it.

God's Gift for Guarding

Nurturing our gifts, or inflaming them into brightness, involves not only recognizing their origins in God's gifting and exercising them in the midst of suffering but also guarding "sound teaching" (1:13). The sound, or healthy, teaching that he mentions was stated in succinct lines in 1 Timothy 3:16 and summarized in an even tidier form in chapter 2, both of which verses I now quote:

> He appeared in the flesh,
>   was vindicated by the Spirit,
> was seen by angels,
>   was preached among the nations,
> was believed on in the world,
>   was taken up in glory. (1 Timothy 3:16)

> Remember Jesus Christ, raised from the dead, descended from David. This is my gospel. (2 Timothy 2:8)

What Timothy is to guard is a message about Jesus Christ—the story into which he fits and the crucial events in his life.

Good guarding means embodying the gospel in one's life and not just in one's words or sermons. Leaders nurture their gifts of teaching when they guard the gospel "with faith and love in Christ Jesus" (1:13). All over again, all is grace: "guard it with the help of the Holy Spirit who lives in us" (1:14).

Nurturing gifts means knowing our location in the body of Christ, a location that snugly sits next to others doing what God called them (not you or me) to do. As Barbara Brown Taylor once reflected, "It was part of God's genius to incorporate us as one body, so that our ears have other ears, other eyes, minds, hearts, and voices to help us interpret what we have heard. Together we hear our calls, and together we can answer them, if only we will listen for the still, small voice that continues to speak to us in the language of our lives" (Taylor, *The Preaching Life*, 25).

QUESTIONS FOR REFLECTION AND APPLICATION

1. What are some differences between human talents and spiritual gifts?

2. What part does laying on of hands play in the distribution of spiritual gifts?

3. How does the Holy Spirit get involved in gifting believers?

4. How does suffering help us nurture our gifts?

5. What spiritual gifts can you nurture in your life?

FOR FURTHER READING

Bonhoeffer, Dietrich. *Life Together* and *Prayerbook of the Bible*. Minneapolis: Fortress, 1996.

Taylor, Barbara Brown. *The Preaching Life: Living Out Your Vocation*. Cambridge: Cowley, 1993.

Kernochan, Sarah, and Howard Smith, dir. *Marjoe*. Cinema 5 Distributing, 1972. https://www.imdb.com/title/tt0068924/.

Manning, Brennan, with John Blasé, *All Is Grace: A Ragamuffin Memoir*. Colorado Springs: Cook, 2011.

LEADERS KNOW RELATIONSHIPS

2 Timothy 1:15–18

[15] You know that everyone in the province of Asia has deserted me, including Phygelus and Hermogenes.

[16] May the Lord show mercy to the household of Onesiphorus, because he often refreshed me and was not ashamed of my chains. [17] On the contrary, when he was in Rome, he searched hard for me until he found me. [18] May the Lord grant that he will find mercy from the Lord on that day! You know very well in how many ways he helped me in Ephesus.

A pastor friend of mine told me that one lesson in leading a church he has come to terms with is that "some of your best friends will desert you" when you least expect it. But Paul evidently did not expect his close workers to abandon him while he was in prison (cf. 4:9–18).

PAIN

Two men of whom we know nothing but names, Phygelus and Hermogenes, have turned away from the apostle in prison.

They were not alone, for Paul says, "Everyone in the province of Asia has deserted me" (1:15). Hyperbole that it is, "everyone" at least expresses that believers from that region who are in his circle of coworkers have chosen not to be identified with the apostle in his suffering.

RELATIONSHIPS

Onesiphorus chose to stick it out with the apostle Paul, but what is meant by his presence would have included not just personal care but also provision of food and drink ("often refreshed me," 1:16) and whatever Paul may have needed. Prison was not the location of a person after a sentence but the location of a person waiting for a trial. This man is a great example of someone who is not ashamed of Paul and his gospel mission (cf. 1:8, 12). In fact, Onesiphorus searched for Paul when he arrived in Rome from Ephesus (1:17). At least in an earlier time in Rome, Paul was under house arrest for two years (Acts 28:30), and during this time he welcomed guests (28:17–28). As Onesiphorus had helped Paul in Ephesus, so now he is helping him in Rome. So impressed was Paul by the man that he wished God's best on him in two ways: "May the Lord show mercy to the household" of the man as well as on him (2 Timothy 1:16, 18).

The NIV entitles today's passage "Examples of Disloyalty and Loyalty." Genuine love and friendship require faithfulness in love, which can be translated as "allegiance" or "loyalty." Faithfulness generates trustworthiness. However, a demand for loyalty—think of the military, think of one's job, think of insecure church leaders, think of some pastors claiming their brand or their church or their reputation—can be a sign of toxicity rather than genuine love and friendship. Loyalty, then, can be either a virtue or a vice. It requires discernment to know the difference. One of the telltale signs of a goodness culture when it comes to loyalty is freedom to disagree as well as pursuit of telling the truth.

Leadership involves relationships with others. Time spent together. Mutual vision-casting. Weeping together and rejoicing together. At times tests of one's love for another person will prompt some to abandon one formerly loved, while others will remain faithful. When the one to whom one is faithful is doing what is right and transparent, such an act of loyalty will line up a person with Onesiphorus. Sadly, many know the sting of disloyalty.

QUESTIONS FOR REFLECTION AND APPLICATION

1. What kind of betrayal and desertion did Paul face?

2. How did God care for Paul through the faithfulness of a friend?

3. In what ways can loyalty function as a virtue and as a vice?

4. Have you ever been betrayed by a ministry partner? What was that like?

5. When have you seen ministry friends show great faithfulness to you?

LEADERS STICK TO JESUS

2 Timothy 2:1–13

¹ *You then, my son, be strong in the grace that is in Christ Jesus.*
² *And the things you have heard me say in the presence of many witnesses entrust to reliable people who will also be qualified to teach others.* ³ *Join with me in suffering, like a good soldier of Christ Jesus.* ⁴ *No one serving as a soldier gets entangled in civilian affairs, but rather tries to please his commanding officer.* ⁵ *Similarly, anyone who competes as an athlete does not receive the victor's crown except by competing according to the rules.* ⁶ *The hardworking farmer should be the first to receive a share of the crops.* ⁷ *Reflect on what I am saying, for the Lord will give you insight into all this.*

⁸ *Remember Jesus Christ, raised from the dead, descended from David. This is my gospel,* ⁹ *for which I am suffering even to the point of being chained like a criminal. But God's word is not chained.* ¹⁰ *Therefore I endure everything for the sake of the elect, that they too may obtain the salvation that is in Christ Jesus, with eternal glory.*

¹¹ *Here is a trustworthy saying:*

> *If we died with him,*
> *we will also live with him;*
> ¹² *if we endure,*
> *we will also reign with him.*

> If *we disown him,*
> *he will also disown us;*
> [13] *if we are faithless,*
> *he remains faithful,*
> *for he cannot disown himself.*

One temptation in leadership is to get lost in the newest, "bestest" idea about leadership. For more than a decade, many of America's megachurches were taken by leadership proposals, by leadership books, and by a leadership culture. I began to hear the young and gifted say they wanted to become a leader. Two decades earlier they would have wanted to become a pastor or a missionary or an evangelist or a professor. I not uncommonly remarked that I wanted to be a "follower" of Jesus because he was the Leader. Most, bless their hearts, said they did too. But their term concerned me.

At the same time, I noticed on websites and blogs preoccupations with theological tribes. To mimic Paul, "I am a Calvinist. I am emerging. I am neo-Anabaptist. I am a progressive. I am an evangelical." There was very little talk, and sometimes nothing, about Jesus. A lot of chatter about the atonement and the Reformation, but Jesus as a person seemed to be absent. You may remember that when the Red Letter Christians made their case, some were offended for a variety of reasons, none of which matter here. What matters is that the Red Letter Christians were preoccupied with Jesus, with what he said and what he did.

The apostle Paul in today's passage calls us to be obsessed with Jesus.

JESUS-GRACE

The NIV has "son" at 2:1, but the term here (*teknon*) is Paul's favorite for those he has disciplined into the way of Jesus. It is best translated as "my child." As a father would to a child, Paul exhorts Timothy to "be strong" or empowered "in the grace that is in Christ Jesus." Grace needs careful understanding because of its importance to Paul—it can serve almost as a synonym for Jesus at times! Many sell grace short when they reduce it to "unmerited favor" or to "getting what you don't deserve." Grace is far more than unmerited favor, but it includes unmerited favor. If we don't include what is involved in grace's "far more," grace is sold short. John Barclay gets it right because he examines the term in the ancient world through the idea of gift. He gives us this dense definition:

> "Gift" denotes the sphere *of voluntary, personal relations, characterized by goodwill in the giving of benefit or favor, and eliciting some form of reciprocal return that is both voluntary and necessary for the continuation of the relationship.* (*Paul and the Gift*, 575)

Here are the important elements of grace: First, it is a relationship established by the Giver (God) with the receiver (us). Second, the "goodwill" in the New Testament is God's love for us that reaches out to us even though we are sinners (unmerited favor). Third, grace given forms a response of gratitude and prompts a person to reciprocate by becoming a gift-giver herself. Finally, when we look at today's passage, *all this grace comes to us in Jesus* and nowhere else. Grace, then, is not a theological system but a person (God) engaged in relationship with a human (us) in the face of Jesus Christ.

Grace empowers us because we know we are loved, that we can now love in turn, and that we are now drawn into a cycle of grace in this world. Paul exhorts Timothy to tell others about Jesus-grace and to pass it on to others, to Jesus-grace-people, who can pass it on and on and on (2:2).

JESUS-LIKE

The Jesus-grace passed on to people who are truly Jesus-people fires Paul's imagination into using metaphors for the lifestyle for those who want to be Jesus-like. Paul says following Jesus entails suffering like a "good soldier" (2:3) because a good soldier is loyal to the "commanding officer," which here is Jesus (2:4). Following Jesus well is like the "athlete" who "competes" by following the contest's rules (2:5), or like a "hardworking farmer" (2:6). And, perhaps with a wink in his eye, Paul tells Timothy if he's having a hard time catching all these Jesus-like analogies, "the Lord will give you insight" if you need it (2:7)—that is, Jesus will show each of us how best to follow him in our way and in our day. That is why I clapped for the Red Letter Christians when they went public: they reminded each of us that leaders need to stick tight with Jesus.

Paul could now be raising his eyebrows to say sticking tight means tight to the cross, not just some idealized good life. In his wonderful talks to Christian leaders in India, Lesslie Newbigin gave a talk called "When I Am Weak, Then I Am Strong." He told those doing ministry that the center of that kind of life is the cross. "The leader is called to actualize in one's life, and to help others to actualize in their lives that total surrender to the will of God which looks like weakness but is indeed the power of God for salvation. I cannot explain this; I can only testify that it is so." He then explained that sometimes this weakness looks like "sheer incapacity" and at other times like "moral and spiritual weakness" because of one's own failures. And this kind of suffering in leadership is not a "dimension" but the very "definition" of what it means to minister to others. "For what is the work of the ministry if not to lead others in following Jesus in the way of the Cross?" (Newbigin, *The Good Shepherd*, 146–47).

JESUS-LIVING

The gospel is the story *about Jesus*. Paul says this in about as simple terms as you will find in the whole New Testament: "Remember Jesus Christ, raised from the dead, descended from David. This is my gospel" (2:8). The gospel not only tells the life and suffering and death and resurrection and ascension of Jesus, but it establishes a template for how we are to live. Notice what Paul chases after as soon as he clarifies the gospel.

First, Jesus-living means suffering in the gospel mission (2:8–9). Second, Paul either composes some poetic lines or he quotes four lines from some early Christian poetry when he writes about Jesus-living in these terms (2:11–13). He begins with positive lines.

#1: If we died with him, we will also live with him.
#2: If we endure, we will also reign with him.

Then he turns to negative possibility.

#3: If we disown him, he will also disown us.

This sounds like Matthew 10:32–33, where Jesus said, "Whoever acknowledges me before others, I will also acknowledge before my Father in heaven. But whoever disowns me before others, I will disown before my Father in heaven." Paul knows that negative line sounds harsh, so he backs up a bit to say,

#4: If we are faithless [or choose not to be allegiant to Christ], he remains faithful, for he cannot disown himself [same word as the words in line #3].

The problem, then, is not God's, and the disowners cannot blame God. God remains faithful.

Jesus-living is a life shaped by the life Jesus himself lived, which means self-denial and surrendering to the will of God. As his life entailed suffering, so Paul tells Timothy that they, too, will suffer (and are suffering!).

Behind the grace of God is Jesus. "Lamb of God, Rose of Sharon, Prince of Peace—none of the things people have found to call him has ever managed to say it quite right. You can see why when he told people to follow him, they often did, even if they backed out later when they started to catch on to what lay ahead" (Buechner, *Beyond Words*, 184). Timothy had more than caught on, but that did not mean he didn't need some encouragement to hang on all over again.

QUESTIONS FOR REFLECTION AND APPLICATION

1. What is different about the way McKnight is using "leader" in this study and the way many church-growth materials and approaches use the word "leader"?

2. How does Barclay's definition of "grace" help you understand the concept better?

3. What happens when Christians stop centering their lives and beliefs on the person and story of Jesus?

4. Have you ever used a red-letter Bible edition? What impact did it have on you?

5. In what ways is your life becoming more Jesus-shaped?

FOR FURTHER READING

Barclay, John M. G. *Paul and the Gift*. Grand Rapids: Eerdmans, 2015.

Buechner, Frederick. *Beyond Words: Daily Readings in the ABC's of Faith*. San Francisco: HarperSanFrancisco, 2004.

Newbigin, Lesslie. *The Good Shepherd: Meditations on Christian Ministry in Today's World*. Grand Rapids: Eerdmans, 1977.

LEADERS GENTLY INSTRUCT

2 Timothy 2:14–26

[14] Keep reminding God's people of these things. Warn them before God against quarreling about words; it is of no value, and only ruins those who listen. [15] Do your best to present yourself to God as one approved, a worker who does not need to be ashamed and who correctly handles the word of truth. [16] Avoid godless chatter, because those who indulge in it will become more and more ungodly. [17] Their teaching will spread like gangrene. Among them are Hymenaeus and Philetus, [18] who have departed from the truth. They say that the resurrection has already taken place, and they destroy the faith of some. [19] Nevertheless, God's solid foundation stands firm, sealed with this inscription: "The Lord knows those who are his," and, "Everyone who confesses the name of the Lord must turn away from wickedness."

[20] In a large house there are articles not only of gold and silver, but also of wood and clay; some are for special purposes and some for common use. [21] Those who cleanse themselves from the latter will be instruments for special purposes, made holy, useful to the Master and prepared to do any good work.

[22] Flee the evil desires of youth and pursue righteousness, faith, love and peace, along with those who call on the Lord out of a pure

heart. *23 Don't have anything to do with foolish and stupid arguments, because you know they produce quarrels. 24 And the Lord's
servant must not be quarrelsome but must be kind to everyone,
able to teach, not resentful. 25 Opponents must be gently instructed,
in the hope that God will grant them repentance leading them to
a knowledge of the truth, 26 and that they will come to their senses
and escape from the trap of the devil, who has taken them captive
to do his will.*

Something in the customary style of Christian preaching
pollutes the style of communication for those influenced
by preaching. We have absorbed into the tissues on our bones
a communication style one might call "didactic." Better yet,
we think we need to be "yellers" and "tellers." The Bible,
let's admit it, does include strong communication, with the
number of commands and prohibitions and prophets and law-
givers and evangelists telling people what to believe and what
to do. Paul's letters are back-loaded with imperatives, and
these letters to leaders have imperatives from beginning to
end. But we sometimes miss another element of the Bible's
own corrective to what has become at times our tendencies
toward a toxic preachy vibe. It is not until the end of today's
passage that this corrective appears, and it reframes and
reshapes everything Paul has said and will say in this letter
to his "child" in the faith, Timothy. So it helps all of us if we
read today's passage backward, beginning with 2:23–26.

GENTLY

In 2 Timothy 2:25 Paul says, "opponents must be *gently*
instructed," (emphasis added). Let's sit with that for a spell
and give it permission to diminish our yelling and telling. Try
reading today's passage aloud (to yourself, not in the coffee
shop) with a gentle, pastoral tone from "Keep reminding" all

the way to "do his will." If you have a mind for it, try now reading it aloud with a preachy tone. Then compare the two. You will immediately feel the difference. The word translated as "gently" is sometimes translated as "meekly," and it suggests a patient, caring, mentoring relationship. Not the prophet standing on the street corner barking out a coming disaster, but a person sitting next to another person and guiding them into the ways of Jesus.

The aim of such gentle instruction is not winning or proving or debunking but the divine gift of "repentance" that will lead them to "truth" and so "escape from the trap of the devil" (2:25–26). Our social media descends often into a call-out culture with the sole aim of conquering and shaming. Paul urges Timothy to nurture a correction culture that mentors a person out of false narratives into the truth. (I'm not saying we are to never call someone out, for there is a time for that.) It appears to me that those who need gentle instruction are not even believers or, if they are, they have seriously wandered from the truth of the gospel. What we do know is that they are described with a graphic word: "opponents" in the NIV translates *anti-dia-tithēmi* as those who place themselves strongly against someone, otherwise, the contradicters or contrarians.

If we now back up, we discover that once again Paul urges the leader to walk away from "foolish and stupid arguments, because you know they produce quarrels," or word wars (2:23). What is said at 2:25 was said at 2:24. The "Lord's servant" is not to be "quarrelsome" and instead is to be "kind to everyone, able to teach, not resentful" (2:24).

You may have leaders in mind who are like this. The person who comes to mind for me is Dallas Willard, whom I heard speak a few times. Dallas had the pastoral, avuncular skill of addressing difficult problems, correcting mistaken ideas, and exhorting us all to walk more in the way of Jesus that crushed us with wisdom. I have upped my gentleness quotient because of him, though I'm nowhere near his level. Instruction is not the only term Paul connects then with "gently." There are four more once we get this communication corrective in verse 25 in place.

Gently Testify

In the need to "keep reminding" everyone of the gospel's basics (2:14a), a leader will need to "warn" with gentleness too (2:14b). Word warring is the problem (NIV: "quarreling about words"). He no doubt—who hasn't experienced this?—has heard about precise definitions and precise corrections and precise formulas. And he has been told about people using words to insult others. The NIV's "warn" is stronger than the term Paul uses here, which is *diamarturomai*, which can be translated as "witness" or "testify." The term describes speaking to them about their word wars but doing so "before God." It is not a rebuke. Rather, the term describes a clear witness to the truth.

Gently Present

What best turns a leader's communications from toxic carping to gentle instruction is the leader's transparency before God (2:15). The leader is to commit to such transparency before God. Katelyn Beaty's recent book about Christian celebrities reflects often on defining celebrity as "social power without proximity" (Beaty, *Celebrities for Jesus*, 17), which involves the paradox of social visibility without proximity. In other words, withdrawing into privacy so that no one really knows you while expanding and extending one's platform and fame. Paul urges God-transparency for Timothy in Ephesus. Not being loud, showy, but living gently.

Notice that Paul immediately connects this life-before-God with a Timothy "who correctly handles the word of truth" (2:15). His image describes someone who cuts a straight path for others to walk. He tells him to pave the way for others by explaining the gospel's truth with wise, compelling clarity, as John R. W. Stott did for his generation. Those who cut straight paths with Scripture will be unashamed workers—that is, people who can stand before God both with gentleness and confidence.

My wish for all leaders is to have mentors like the apostle Paul.

GENTLY AVOID

Paul's term translated "avoid" pictures standing around or outside a meaningless, profitless, unedifying "godless chatter" (2:16). Some want to barge right into the battle. The wise gently maintain a distance and walk around the circle of contention. It's so easy to drop a nasty into Twitter's comment box, and it's not unusual to feel bad and wish we hadn't done the dropping. Two different terms describe the corrupt teaching. The first is "godless," which translates *bebēlos*, and I prefer the translation "populist." The second is "ungodly" and, because it is the opposite of "civilized piety" (*eusebeia*), a good suggestion is "uncivilized piety" (*asebeia*). He imagines people claiming religious expertise but acting like a fool in public.

The consequence for this circle of corrupt teachers is the destruction of the faith of others. The teachings "spread like gangrene" (2:17), and he spells out one element of the corrupted theology: they "say that the resurrection has already taken place" (2:18). The Christian teaching about the resurrection affirms that your body will rise from a physical grave and be reconstituted for an eternal life. As N. T. Wright has often said, resurrection does not mean "life after death" but an embodied "life after life after death" (Wright, *Surprised by Hope*, 148).

"Gentle avoiding" anchors both its gentleness and its avoiding in knowing that our God "knows those who are his" (2:19) and they know what their callings are (2:20–21). The leaders who grip the truth of the resurrection are urged with Timothy to "turn away from wickedness" (2:19).

FLEE AND CHASE

Turning away from wickedness, or "flee the evil desires of youth" (2:22), converts one's desires from this world's provisions to two realities: First, one is to "pursue" or chase gently the eternal virtues of "righteousness, faith, love and peace" (2:22). And, second, one is to chase gently after these virtues in the context of a faith community—that is, following Jesus along "with those who call on the Lord out of a pure heart" (2:22).

Let's back up to the word "gently" one more time. Notice what happens to these dynamic words in today's passage when we turn them from loud yelling and telling into gentle actions of the one who wants to mentor the wandering back onto the path: gently testify, gently present oneself, gently walk around the debates, and gently pursue the eternal virtues in the context of a community. "Gently" matters.

QUESTIONS FOR REFLECTION AND APPLICATION

1. What impact does it have to read this section "backward"?

2. What might a correction culture that doesn't shame people look like?

3. How does "uncivilized piety" show up in the culture Paul is writing about and in our culture today?

4. How do you feel about preachers who "yell and tell"?

5. In what areas of your life could you cultivate more gentleness?

FOR FURTHER READING

Beaty, Katelyn. *Celebrities for Jesus: How Personas, Platforms, and Profits Are Hurting the Church.* Grand Rapids: Brazos, 2022.

Wright, N. T. *Surprised by Hope: Rethinking Heaven, the Resurrection, and the Mission of the Church.* New York: HarperOne, 2008.

LEADERS DISCERN THE MORAL CONDITIONS

2 Timothy 3:1–9

¹ But mark this: There will be terrible times in the last days. ² People will be lovers of themselves, lovers of money, boastful, proud, abusive, disobedient to their parents, ungrateful, unholy, ³ without love, unforgiving, slanderous, without self-control, brutal, not lovers of the good, ⁴ treacherous, rash, conceited, lovers of pleasure rather than lovers of God— ⁵ having a form of godliness but denying its power. Have nothing to do with such people.

⁶ They are the kind who worm their way into homes and gain control over gullible women, who are loaded down with sins and are swayed by all kinds of evil desires, ⁷ always learning but never able to come to a knowledge of the truth. ⁸ Just as Jannes and Jambres opposed Moses, so also these teachers oppose the truth. They are men of depraved minds, who, as far as the faith is concerned, are rejected. ⁹ But they will not get very far because, as in the case of those men, their folly will be clear to everyone.

History is going somewhere, and some of those "somewheres" are disasters pointing us toward a final act of God to eliminate evil and to establish peace with justice and love in the final kingdom. Church history reveals that when Christian leaders keep their wits about them, they perceive stunningly helpful signs as they observe the moral conditions of a society. When they don't keep their wits about them, they tend toward foolish and reckless speculations. Those with their wits learn to distinguish what we *can* know from what we *cannot* know. What we cannot know is *when*. What we can know is *potential indicators of the final kingdom*.

The rule is stated in 3:1: history's "last days" will be marked by "terrible times," or what could be translated as "dangerous seasons." Not all terrible times are the last days, and those with discernment avoid jumping to conclusions. Since "terrible times" can lead to a myriad of interpretations, it is wise for us to read what Paul says about those "terrible times" that could be indicators of the "last times." Three indicators of the last times are mentioned. Once again, the last times will certainly be marked by the three indicators in the following sections, but these noticeable traits do not always indicate the last times.

One final bit worth considering: since the founding of the United States, various preachers and authors have gone on record predicting the imminent demise of the country, of society, and even of the world. Often such speculators used the very verses we are about to look at more closely. Such speculations *have been wrong every time* because they did not distinguish between *potential* and *certain* indicators (see Mathewes and Nichols, *Prophesies of Godlessness*). Here's what I have learned, and this after listening to one or two decades of preachers and authors predicting the end of the world: we are far better at discerning corruption than predicting the future. Here are three moral conditions that can indicate the "last days." One of the responsibilities of leaders in Christian communities is to discern moral conditions.

MORAL DEGRADATION

Paul's list is a scattershot graphic of moral degradation. I will translate the terms to give the list of 3:2–4 a freshness: "self-lovers, silver-lovers, braggarts, status-mongers, insulters, unpersuaded by parents, ungracious, unsaintly, unloving, unrelenting, accusers, uncontrolled, untamed, unfriendly-with-good, traitors, precipitous, puffed up, lovers-of-pleasure rather than lovers-of-God" (from my *The Second Testament*). We can all agree this list points at unvirtuous behaviors and character, but we can all also agree such corruptions have been with us always—but they will be more intense in the last days.

Many of us grew up hearing that the world was getting worse and worse, and since the currents we perceive in our world are worse than ever, the end was near. If you want to focus on crime and drug proliferation in the USA, times don't look good. (We do not need to equate the USA with the world, however.) But if you study progress of some basics about life in the world, like food or sanitation or life expectancy or the environment or literacy or freedom, you will hear the other side of the story (Norberg, *Progress*; Rosling, *Factfulness*). This undeniable other side of the story reveals that the "last days" are actually not here.

Yet we can't simply dismiss discernment as a game for looney birds. Like Paul, like Timothy, like others, we need to be morally discerning of our times. Each generation and each nation will vary from one another about what it discerns. That is, we *can* know moral conditions, whether we think they are signs of the "last days" or not. For instance, more humans have died in wars, either from warfare or refugee deaths, in the last century than any time in history. That's bad. Ministers are collapsing morally at a rate that alarms most of us. An increasing number of young adults who were nurtured at home and in the church are now becoming what is called the "Nones"—that is, those who when asked what their faith is or their church is answer "None" (Smietana, *Reorganized Religion*). The issue here is not just the number of Nones but also why they are walking away from organized religion.

SPIRITUAL POVERTY

In one quick line Paul summarizes a massive problem. The corrupted people Paul has in mind exhibit "a form of godliness but denying its power" (3:5). Now our understanding of the word "godliness" becomes the deciding element in understanding what Paul is saying. The Greek term is *eusebeia*, which is about civilized piety or socially respectable religious behaviors. Paul knows of people who desire the honors and notoriety for a socially respectable religion but who have nothing to do with the "power" that unleashes an authentic Christian faith in publicly observable behaviors. Even more, the emphasis is on a public religion that lacks continuity with the gospel and the Christian community.

The jolt comes when we combine *eusebeia* with the behaviors of verses 2 through 4. How, you and I will naturally ask, can people desire honor for their professions but behind closed doors act abusively and proudly and greedily? Such people wear a spiritual mask.

No wonder Paul urges Timothy to walk around and by such people (3:5b). Discerning people learn who needs to be avoided when it comes to Christian community spiritual formation. Let me say it: the Nones, mentioned previously, are telling us why many today are abandoning organized church life. Why? Because of the spiritual poverty of many leaders and churches.

CHURCH MANIPULATION

The problem is, false teachers "worm their way into [house churches] and gain control over [little women]" (3:6). The word translated with "gullible" narrows what Paul wrote. He uses the diminutive form of "woman," thereby indicating that the problem is their spiritual and theological maturity. To use "gullible" could suggest to many (and does!) that women are (1) gullible and (2) less rational and (3) more emotional and therefore (4) less reliable than men. A good parallel to this then is what Paul wrote to Timothy in the first letter (1 Timothy 5:11–15 and then also 2:11–14). The "little" women Paul has in mind are morally immature as well in that they are "loaded down with sins and are swayed by all kinds of evil desires" (2 Timothy 3:6). We need to connect this passage tightly to 1 Timothy 5. The women in mind are "always 'learning' [added irony] but never able to come to a knowledge of the truth" (3:7).

Descriptions like these say a lot without telling readers some twenty centuries later who these women might be. There are a variety of suggestions, none of which are off base, each of which has advocates, and none of which has convinced all those who study the contexts carefully. The women appear to be wealthy, curious, and conscious of appearance and social status. They are also described as lacking spiritual and theological maturity and as disrupting the house churches of Ephesus. They have been duped by false teachers. Paul compares the false teachers to the Old Testament examples of "Jannes and Jambres" (3:8), who became the archnames of those who opposed Moses in texts like Exodus 7:8–13 and probably Numbers 22:22, though they are not named there. Connecting the false teachers who worm their way into house churches to Jannes and Jambres is one of Paul's put-downs or slurs. The false teachers at Ephesus have "depraved minds" (3:8), and they are outside gospel faith.

Eventually their stories will become "clear to everyone" (3:9). Paul's sentence is dense and can be translated like this: "For their ignorance will be very clear to all—as also the ignorance of these [Jannes and Jambres] men became [clear]." Eventually the truth will win, and that's good news on which to end today's passage.

To back up: we may know the *what* of moral degradation, spiritual poverty, and church manipulation in our world today. These *may* indicate we are nearing the end times, but the *when* we don't know. Neither did Jesus. In these times we are called to discern the moral conditions, to walk with Jesus, and to warn those in the church who are failing us.

QUESTIONS FOR REFLECTION AND APPLICATION

1. How does Paul guide Timothy to discern the times?

2. What indicators of the last days that Paul gives Timothy do you see around you today?

3. In what ways do false teachers cause people to leave the church and the faith?

4. What do you think are the major marks of moral corruptions today?

5. How do you use discernment to interact wisely with the world around you?

FOR FURTHER READING

Mathewes, Charles, and Christopher McKnight Nichols. *Prophesies of Godlessness: Predictions of America's Imminent Secularization from the Puritans to the Present Day*. New York: Oxford University Press, 2008.

Norberg, Johan. *Progress: Ten Reasons to Look Forward to the Future*. London: Oneworld, 2017.

Rosling, Hans. *Factfulness: Ten Reasons We're Wrong about the World—And Why Things are Better Than You Think*. New York: Flatiron, 2018.

Smietana, Bob. *Reorganized Religion: The Reshaping of the American Church and Why It Matters*. New York: Worthy, 2022.

LEADERS LEAD THROUGH LIFE AND SCRIPTURE

2 Timothy 3:10–4:5

¹⁰ You, however, know all about my teaching, my way of life, my purpose, faith, patience, love, endurance, ¹¹ persecutions, sufferings—what kinds of things happened to me in Antioch, Iconium and Lystra, the persecutions I endured. Yet the Lord rescued me from all of them. ¹² In fact, everyone who wants to live a godly life in Christ Jesus will be persecuted, ¹³ while evildoers and impostors will go from bad to worse, deceiving and being deceived. ¹⁴ But as for you, continue in what you have learned and have become convinced of, because you know those from whom you learned it, ¹⁵ and how from infancy you have known the Holy Scriptures, which are able to make you wise for salvation through faith in Christ Jesus. ¹⁶ All Scripture is God-breathed and is useful for teaching, rebuking, correcting and training in righteousness, ¹⁷ so that the servant of God may be thoroughly equipped for every good work.

^{4:1} In the presence of God and of Christ Jesus, who will judge the living and the dead, and in view of his appearing and his kingdom, I give you this charge: ² Preach the word; be prepared in season and

out of season; correct, rebuke and encourage—with great patience and careful instruction. ³ For the time will come when people will not put up with sound doctrine. Instead, to suit their own desires, they will gather around them a great number of teachers to say what their itching ears want to hear. ⁴ They will turn their ears away from the truth and turn aside to myths. ⁵ But you, keep your head in all situations, endure hardship, do the work of an evangelist, discharge all the duties of your ministry.

This letter winds two threads together: the thread of Paul's own journey and the thread of Timothy's journey. Paul winds his thread around Timothy's to mentor him into the way of the gospel in the house churches of Ephesus. But the winding continues: we hear about Paul's own life often in this letter (1:3–5, 8, 11–12, 13, 15–18; 2:2–3, 9–10), but not so Paul can talk about himself. We hear about him only because Paul wants his life to impact Timothy's. As well, we hear about Timothy's life only because Paul wants it to conform to the gospel about Jesus Christ. The most effective form of mentoring another person says "Come walk with me, come watch me, and come learn the way of Jesus with me. Let us learn this way together." Education in the ancient world was always about emulation more than information, about imitation more than about intellectual grasp. Both information and emulation are needed, but without a life witnessing to that information, the information becomes dull, sterile, and proud. The mentor who follows Jesus well makes the information humble because the mentor embodies it in a way that does not say "Look at me!" but "Look at Jesus as you walk with me in his way."

Leaders walk the path alongside, slightly ahead, and at times behind others. But in walking they become conscious that they are setting an example. They don't make the way. The Way has been made by the one who is the Way. Leaders follow the Way because Jesus is ahead, but leaders invite others to join them on that Way. They lead others, first, by sharing their life.

LEADERS SHARE THEIR LIFE

Leading on this Way begins with transparent claims: "You, however, know all about *my* . . ." and I'll stop right there before we get to what that "my" is all about. What Paul knows is that Timothy knows him. Pastors have told me for years that they have learned "to trust very few but pastor all." Others smother their trust all over the room and get smothered by betrayal in turn. Whether you share your heart with many or with few, sharing your heart determines your health as a leader. Every leader needs mentors whom they trust, with whom they can express their feelings and fears, to whom they can surrender their ideas for wisdom—and listening to the mentor shapes the heart of the leader. I'm not talking friends here. I'm talking mentors. Someone ahead of you on the path who knows the path you are to take and can advise without preaching and demanding and controlling. Wise mentors, like Paul, guide but don't domineer.

"You, however, know all about my teaching, my way of life, my purpose" and here the NIV unfortunately drops "my." There is, yes, only one "my" in the Greek text, and it occurs before "teaching," but its location before teaching means it applies to the whole list, so I continue: "[my] faith, [my] patience, [my] love, [my] endurance, [my] persecutions, [my] sufferings" (3:10–11). Timothy witnessed some of this, but Paul told him about what Timothy did not observe, which means Paul was transparent about his life with Timothy, which means (and this is not here) Timothy shared his life with those he mentored.

Paul suffered often. Read 2 Corinthians 11:21–33. The

man must have been known for sores, scars, and bloodstains. From it all he learned this: "everyone who wants to live a godly life in Christ Jesus will be persecuted" (2 Timothy 3:12). Here "godly" means the one living a socially respectable life will discover at times that the cutting edge of the gospel's claims will be repudiated, rejected, and persecuted.

But mentoring others is not just about sharing our life as something about us. It's not about us. It's about Jesus Christ, and our story works only when it leads others to follow Jesus. The wise, widely experienced pastor-professor William Willimon once said,

> It is not my task primarily to "share myself" with my people, certainly not to heed the facile advice of those who say, "Just be yourself." (As Mark Twain said, that's about the worst advice one can give anybody.) Fortunately, as I enter into the struggles of my people, I have considerably more to offer than myself. I have the witness of the saints, the faith of the church, the wisdom of the ages. (Willimon, *Pastor*, 21)

A different colored thread woven through this letter represents the opponents of the gospel in Ephesus, some of whom are defectors from the gospel. Paul labels them here as "evildoers and impostors" and tells Timothy what he already knows: they will keep on doing what such people do—"deceiving and being deceived" (3:13). Mentor Paul is no idealist who thinks everyone will believe and behave. The newish leader will learn that Christians can be mean, that some will betray them, that others will fight against them and spread gossip and rumors and lies. The idealism of newish leadership gives way to the realism of maturish leadership when we come to terms with the sinfulness of all.

Leaders in the way of Jesus lead not only by sharing their

life with others but also by soaking in Scripture and leading others by teaching Scripture.

LEADERS READ THE SCRIPTURE

Many leaders have the experience of Timothy: he had a mentor and a spiritually mature mother and grandmother (3:14). All Paul mentions here is "from whom you learned"—that is, his grandmother Lois and his mother Eunice (1:5). One can assume that they both had joined with others who were on the Way with Jesus prior to Timothy, but their faith (1:5; 3:14 *pistoō* cognate to believe/faith) derived from their Jewish past. As faithful Jewish women, they taught Timothy "the Holy Scriptures"—that is, our Old Testament (3:15). He was mentored into the faith by two women before he was mentored as a gospel agent by the apostle Paul.

The heart of this mentoring was to know both the content and power of the Scriptures, "which are able to make you wise for salvation through faith in Christ Jesus" (3:15). In the Scriptures one learns the story of God, its truthfulness affirmed because it is "God-breathed" (3:16), an expression that has historically been translated with "inspired." The NIV translates the word literally (*theo* + *pneustos* = God + spirit-ed or breathed).

Because the Scriptures derive in that manner from God, the Scriptures are useful for four dimensions of spiritual formation: first, Scriptures teach us the gospel; second, Scriptures rebuke or convict us when we are out of line; third, Scriptures can straighten us out again; and, fourth, Scriptures educate us in the will of God so that we can walk in "righteousness" (3:16). These four dimensions are the content of Scripture. Deriving as they do from the good, loving, holy, and righteous God, the power of God's Spirit is at work in our encounters with Scripture so that "the servant of God [in our

139

theme, leaders] may be thoroughly equipped for every good work" (3:17). That is, so we can develop a publicly visible civilized life that conforms to the Way of Jesus as it becomes respectable to others (within limits, of course).

Those called to lead in the church at any level will gain from daily reading of the Bible. Many read the Bible through in a year by reading four chapters per day (with room to miss some days), others cut that reading in half and read the Bible in two years. Some like to read from one and only one (their favorite) translation, while others like to read from various translations. Some read the Old Testament through on a two-year plan while they read the New Testament every year, while yet others zero in on one book or one author (say Matthew, or Luke and Acts, or the Pauline letters). What matters is that routine Bible reading puts a person in the position of hearing from God if that person puts oneself in the posture of listening for God to speak. The aim is not to master the content so one can know everything about the Bible and answer on-the-spot Bible trivia. No, the aim is to be mastered by God, who speaks to us through God-spirited Scripture. What we want most is to hear from God and for that encounter to transform us into agents of "every good work" (3:17).

LEADERS ANNOUNCE THE WORD

The threads of the lives of Timothy and Paul weave another turn. In the most sacred of terms, Paul gives a witness to his mentee. First, what he says is made "in the presence of God" and in the presence of "Jesus Christ," and the one before whom he is about to utter his sacred charge "will judge the living and the dead" (4:1). Second, this same Jesus is coming again and, third, when Jesus returns, the "kingdom" will arrive in its fullness. Paul can't be more serious about his "charge," or witness.

The charge is simple: "Preach the word" (4:2). With that word "preach," we may say "I'm not a preacher, so this is not for me." Hold on a second. The word means "to announce" or "declare," and what Paul has in mind is not Sunday morning's sermon time. It has to do with a leader bringing the gospel about Jesus into her leadership, and entering Jesus into our ways will involve, first, an all-the-time guidance or even superintendence ("in season and out of season"). Second, this all-the-time Jesus may involve correcting, rebuking, and encouraging—but not harping and carping. No, Paul advises Timothy to be an all-the-time Jesus person "with great patience and careful instruction" (4:2). Don't get hung up on the word "careful" because it's not in the Greek text. What is present is "all," and it applies to patience and teaching, which means he wants Timothy to be an all-the-time Jesus kind of leader. He'd say the same to you and me.

Remember the "terrible times in the last days" of 3:1? They appear again in 4:3 with "For the time will come when people will not put up with sound doctrine." In my corner of the world, I sense this at times. The American churches today are not as theologically sound as they could be, and, frankly, at times I hear pastors who don't seem to care. I wonder if they are leading the charge of those mentioned in 4:3, who, sadly, don't give a hoot or root for "sound doctrine." They don't read the best books, they demean seminary education, they ridicule those who read the Bible in original languages, they pander to the latest theory about leadership and organization, and they cater constantly to social media. I know there are pockets of preachers and leaders who care deeply about healthy theology, but I'm dismayed by those who don't care. Paul's looking at them too when he says these words, and his words are potent, so read them slowly: "to suit their own desires, they will gather around them a great number of teachers to say what their itching ears want to hear. They will turn their ears away from the truth and turn aside to myths" (4:3–4). Update those words here and there and you're looking at the American church. (Names omitted.) Our situation sounds a bit like the one the old pastor faced in Marilynne Robinson's novel *Gilead*, writing out for his son a sigh about what can happen when nonsensical theology takes root in a church: "You can spend forty years teaching people to be awake to the fact of mystery and then some fellow with no more theological sense than a jackrabbit gets himself a radio ministry and all your work is forgotten. I do wonder where it will end" (Robinson, *Gilead*, 208).

Because leaders are to soak in Scripture and to be all-the-time Jesus, Paul says, "Keep your head" (4:5), or be sober in all matters. Knowing Paul's story, Timothy is not one bit surprised by the theme of suffering: "endure hardship." As an all-the-time Jesus leader, he is also to "do the work of an evangelist" and in all things to know his sacred calling as a gospel agent and leader to "discharge all the duties" of his calling (4:5).

QUESTIONS FOR REFLECTION AND APPLICATION

1. Why does Paul talk about himself and his own life in his letters to Timothy?

2. How was education in the ancient world different from education today?

3. How does Scripture function in our spiritual formation?

4. Do you have a Bible-reading plan or approach? If not, what do you think of the ideas presented in this section?

5. Do you see church leaders around you who seem not to care? What might Paul say to them?

FOR FURTHER READING

Robinson, Marilynne. *Gilead: A Novel.* New York: Farrar Straus and Giroux, 2004.
Willimon, William H. *Pastor: The Theology and Practice of Ordained Ministry.* Rev. ed. Nashville: Abingdon, 2016.

LEADERS MODEL HOPE IN ORDINARY LIFE

2 Timothy 4:6–22

⁶ For I am already being poured out like a drink offering, and the time for my departure is near. ⁷ I have fought the good fight, I have finished the race, I have kept the faith. ⁸ Now there is in store for me the crown of righteousness, which the Lord, the righteous Judge, will award to me on that day—and not only to me, but also to all who have longed for his appearing.

⁹ Do your best to come to me quickly, ¹⁰ for Demas, because he loved this world, has deserted me and has gone to Thessalonica. Crescens has gone to Galatia, and Titus to Dalmatia. ¹¹ Only Luke is with me. Get Mark and bring him with you, because he is helpful to me in my ministry. ¹² I sent Tychicus to Ephesus. ¹³ When you come, bring the cloak that I left with Carpus at Troas, and my scrolls, especially the parchments.

¹⁴ Alexander the metalworker did me a great deal of harm. The Lord will repay him for what he has done. ¹⁵ You too should be on your guard against him, because he strongly opposed our message.

¹⁶ At my first defense, no one came to my support, but everyone

deserted me. May it not be held against them. [17] *But the Lord stood at my side and gave me strength, so that through me the message might be fully proclaimed and all the Gentiles might hear it. And I was delivered from the lion's mouth.* [18] *The Lord will rescue me from every evil attack and will bring me safely to his heavenly kingdom. To him be glory for ever and ever. Amen.*

[19] *Greet Priscilla and Aquila and the household of Onesiphorus.* [20] *Erastus stayed in Corinth, and I left Trophimus sick in Miletus.* [21] *Do your best to get here before winter. Eubulus greets you, and so do Pudens, Linus, Claudia and all the brothers and sisters.*

[22] *The Lord be with your spirit. Grace be with you all.*

Paul, knowing his martyrdom was imminent, like Jesus, not only knew of ultimate entrance into the eternal life-giving hands of God but also took care for those he loved. Our passage goes back and forth from a leader's ultimate hope in the resurrection to a leader's common realities. Our resurrection hope becomes most meaningful in the ordinary aspects of our lives. Quotidian chores are buoyed by transcendent hope. Our weaknesses, struggles, and sufferings are sacraments of eternal life.

Yet the confident hope of Paul is not always ours, and frankly, some of our most treasured leaders don't always possess it. We join then with Frederick Buechner, who once said; "As much as it is our hope, it is our hopelessness that brings us to church on a Sunday, and any preacher who, whatever else he speaks, does not speak to that hopelessness might as well save his breath" (Buechner, *Telling the Truth*, 55). Let us not assume or require that leaders are as buoyant in their hope as the apostle Paul. But also let us not surrender the maturation that leads to a "proper confidence," an expression I latched onto long ago when reading Lesslie Newbigin's book *A Proper Confidence*. Paul's hope here models a proper confidence.

A Leader's Confident Hope,
Part 1

As Paul tells more bits about his own story, we sense his story is lost in the larger story of God. The metaphor of "being poured out like a drink offering," when combined with "the time of my departure" (4:6) makes clear that Paul knows his death is at hand. He will die at the hands of a Roman executioner. The phrase "poured out" could be translated in a more active sense with "I am already poured out" or, as in the NIV, in a more passive sense with "I am . . . *being* poured out" (emphasis added).

Readers of the Psalms may at times be annoyed with the confidence of the one praying. That is, the one praying says versions of "deliver me because I deserve it on the basis of following your law." That can strike us as a smudge of self-righteousness, but it's not. It's the honest prayer of the person pleading with God. Paul here claims something similar: "I have fought the good fight, I have finished the race, I have kept the faith" (4:7). The first may evoke soldiering, and the second athletic competition. Paul combined those two images two chapters back (2:3–5). The two—soldiering, running—give metaphors to "I have kept the faith" (4:7). To keep the faith transfers a common expression in Paul's Jewish life: as he had observed the law, so he now observes the faith. Yet, as many have commented, he was enabled to keep it because he was kept by God. Leaders lead by example, especially so as they face death.

How do we best restate what Paul said without getting close to the line as he magnifies the athletic image of verse 7? Because he has been faithful, Paul knows "there is in store for" him the "crown of righteousness" (4:8). The "righteous Judge," the Lord Jesus, will award him that crown. The word "righteous" describes someone who has been faithful in conforming their life to the will of God, and for Paul that standard is the Way of Jesus. The faithful can speak of a reward without claiming any sense of merit; the faithful know they are faithful because God is faithful (cf. 2:13). Unlike athletic races where there is but one winner, the same award given to Paul will be given "to all who have longed for his appearing" (4:8). Here he uses *epiphaneia*, like our word "epiphany," behind "appearing."

Countless leaders face death—due to martyrdom, diseases, aging—in the hope of the resurrection. A faithful life participates in Christ's life, in his death, and in his resurrection. Such a life comes to expression in everyday experiences, to which Paul now turns.

A LEADER'S NEEDS

Leaders have needs too. If we could get to where we don't put our church leaders on pedestals and where our leaders can be honest with us, we would experience the freshness of leaders expressing their needs as Paul does here and not feeling ashamed of it. And we would also experience the joy of providing for our leaders. Our leaders need personal time, family time, relaxation time, preparation time, study time— and they need food and fun and vacation. We have too high of expectations and too low of a sense of responsibility for their care. Burnout is common among pastors, and no small part of that flows directly from high expectations and impossible abilities to meet all of them.

In chains awaiting a verdict and its consequences, which for Paul was death, Paul wanted some company, and here Paul provides an opportunity for us to ponder a leader's common needs. He evokes loneliness when he urges Timothy to "come to me quickly" (4:9) and "only Luke is with me" (4:11). Confident hope in the face of death will not easily erase our need for love and companionship. That loneliness was complicated by a man named Demas, who returned to Thessalonica "because he loved the world" (4:10). Sometimes leaders have close workers who need to be gone, like Crescens and Titus (the recipient of the third pastoral epistle) and Tychicus (4:10, 12). But Paul describes Demas's departure as an abandonment, not a simple leaving, which indicates that one of his close coworkers in the mission had abandoned the faith. Leaders learn they need faithful friends. His need for friendship prompts Paul to ask Timothy to get Mark to accompany him as he comes to Paul (4:11).

Prison time meant waiting for a verdict. Imprisonment was not a sentence (as it is in our world). But the prison officials in most cases did not provide for their prisoners, so Paul needed someone to provide what he needed, which emphasizes for us why Christian compassion often extended to visiting prisoners (cf. Matthew 25:31–46). Paul's imprisonment when he wrote this letter must have been in the cooler seasons because he asks for a "cloak," and (like many of us) he wanted something to read. He asks Timothy to bring "my scrolls, especially the parchments" (4:13), which may have been copies of his letters or even books of the Bible. We could imagine, too, his own notebooks of ideas he had been recording throughout his mission work.

A Leader's Confident Hope, Part 2

Hope blooms most noticeably in the midst of suffering. Paul names some of his own suffering (4:14–18). First, he names "Alexander the metalworker," and it's easy to think he is the same Alexander as in Acts 19:33. Regardless, he inflicted some bad stuff on Paul, and because Paul was confident that he was in the right and doing God's work, he expresses in harsh terms his wish for God to judge Alexander (2 Timothy 4:14) and warns Timothy to keep an eye on him (4:15).

Second, his loneliness appears again in "At my first defense, no one came to my support, but everyone deserted me" (4:16). Remember, Paul didn't have the Backstreet Boys song to keep him company ("Show Me the Meaning of Being Lonely"). We don't know for sure which "first defense" this may have been, but it could have been in Caesarea (Acts 21:27–26:32) or more likely in Rome (28:16–31). Or perhaps this is a first defense in his most recent trial with a second one looming with little chance of survival. "No one" is his coworkers, evidently, because he prays the Lord will not judge them for their desertions (4:16). A pastor friend told me not long ago that one of his most difficult lessons in leading derived from the experience of opposition and even betrayal of personal trust by those who he had thought, were closest to him.

Opposition from those against the faith and desertion by those inside the faith not only exacerbated Paul's loneliness and suffering, but those sufferings provoked his hope into action. "The Lord," the one who was nearly all alone in his trial and on the cross, that Lord "stood at my side and gave me strength" (4:17). God sustained this man's life so he could gospel the inner courts of Rome, and he was "delivered from the lion's mouth" (4:17). I take this to refer to Paul's release from the trial we read about in Acts 28. That release propelled Paul to announce that "the Lord will rescue me from every evil attack," which in some sense did not pan out literally, but what did pan out is what he said next: "and will bring me safely to his heavenly kingdom" (2 Timothy 4:18). These words remind us of what he said earlier in today's passage at 4:8.

Leaders know suffering, and leaders know confident hope, but the latter in the midst of the former is the work of God—and so Paul utters what we find in many of his letter endings, a doxology: "To him be glory for ever and ever" (4:18; cf. Romans 16:25–27; Philippians 4:20; 1 Timothy 6:16).

A LEADER'S FINAL WORDS

Paul's letters, which are often like other letters in the world of Paul, end with greetings and a few personal details and a wish-prayer. He asks Timothy to greet his good friends Priscilla and Aquila and Onesiphorus, catches him up on news about Erastus (Acts 19:22; 1 Corinthians 16:23) and Trophimus (Acts 20:4; 21:29), and gives greetings from Eubulus, Pudens, Linus, Claudia, and "all the brothers and sisters" (4:21). Again, Paul urges Timothy to come quickly (4:21 and 4:9).

Two wish-prayers close this letter from Timothy's mentor: "The Lord be with your spirit" and "Grace be with you all." That little "all" at the end might surprise because it suddenly indicates that this letter is not just for Timothy but also for those he will mentor and, perhaps also, for the churches in their care.

QUESTIONS FOR REFLECTION AND APPLICATION

1. How do you think Paul's impending death might have impacted his writing of this letter to Timothy?

2. Compare how Paul tells his story in light of what God is doing in 1 Timothy 1:12–20; 2 Timothy 1:11–12; 2:8–13; and 4:6–8.

3. Crowns often describe God's final evaluation: 1 Thessalonians 2:19; James 1:12; 1 Peter 5:4; and Revelation 2:10. List the word used with "crown of" and ponder what each says about the nature of Christian living and hope.

4. What are you doing and what is your church doing to listen to the needs of your leaders and to help meet those needs? Do your leaders feel safe enough to express their needs to other leaders and to the church?

5. If you knew you would die soon, what would you write to your mentees?

FOR FURTHER READING

Backstreet Boys, "Show Me the Meaning of Being Lonely," on the album *Millennium*. Legacy Recordings, 2019.

Buechner, Frederick. *Telling the Truth: The Gospels as Tragedy, Comedy, and Fairy Tale*. San Francisco: Harper & Row, 1977.

Newbigin, Lesslie. *A Proper Confidence: Faith, Doubt, and Certainty in Christian Discipleship*. Grand Rapids: Eerdmans, 1995.

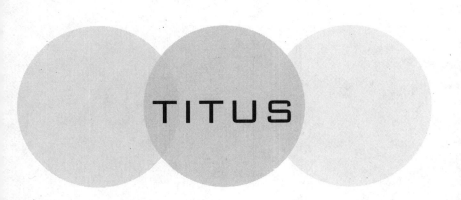

TITUS

LEADERS BEGIN WELL

Titus 1:1–4

¹ Paul, a servant of God and an apostle of Jesus Christ to further the faith of God's elect and their knowledge of the truth that leads to godliness— ² in the hope of eternal life, which God, who does not lie, promised before the beginning of time, ³ and which now at his appointed season he has brought to light through the preaching entrusted to me by the command of God our Savior,

⁴ To Titus, my true son in our common faith.

Grace and peace from God the Father and Christ Jesus our Savior.

Because we have read them before, the opening few verses of each of the New Testament letters sound so familiar that we may choose to hurry over them to get to the meat of the letter itself. Mind you, skipping someone's well-chosen words dismisses them as a person because words are God's way of communicating with us and the way we communicate with one another. To listen to another person loves them; to dismiss their words devalues the person. When someone opens a session or a speech or a sermon or a letter or an introduction with customary words, we might pause to consider why such words have been so customary.

In Paul's so-called greeting (1:1–4), he enters into a relationship with Titus by (1) identifying himself, (2) naming the relationship this apostle has with Titus, and (3) providing a wish-prayer for Titus to experience the "grace and peace" that alone comes from God. Titus, by listening carefully to Paul's letter, is drawn into the gospel mission of God given to Paul. Their relationship is mission shaped. Leaders know their calling and their mission, and it shapes relationships. But I must back off for a moment to say leaders remain people, persons who know God and who are called to follow Jesus, and their personal relationship with Jesus is more important than their calling and mission and gifting. Their personal relationships matter before their calling matters. As long as the personal relationships come first, the leader's mission can frame relationships with others. As Paul's did with Titus.

Titus: A Sketch of His Life

Unfortunately, Titus is never mentioned in Acts. He was a Greek convert, became a serious disciple of Jesus, and then became a mission agent with Paul and Barnabas.

His time with Paul in Galatians 2:1–10 corresponds to the famine visit of Paul and Barnabas recorded in Acts 11:27–30. Titus accompanied them to Jerusalem, where he witnessed indications of both the tensions and the unity of the church. As a young convert and mission agent, he observed tensions of whether gentile believers ought to be circumcised to be part of the church (Galatians 2:4). The result of the meeting was an apparent cooperation between

the missions of Peter and Paul (2:9). He probably
returned with Paul to Antioch (Acts 13:1).

There is no indication he accompanied Paul
and Barnabas on the first and second missionary
trips (Acts 12:25/13:4–14:28; 15:36–18:22), but
he does travel with Paul on the third mission trip
(13:23–21:16), and thus Titus participated in Paul's
relentless raising of funds for the saints in Jerusalem.

We hear about Titus next in Crete (Titus 1:4),
then probably he traveled to be with Paul on the north-
west coast of Greece in Nicopolis (3:12), and then we
hear he has moved on to Dalmatia (2 Timothy 4:10).

Paul begins this letter by defining his calling's relationship with Titus's calling, and both of these are wrapped up
in an intensive personal relationship with God and with one
another.

LEADERS BEGIN WELL BY
RECOGNIZING RELATIONSHIPS

This letter starts with customary words because customary
words bring to expression the wisdom of the ages for how a
letter ought to begin. Knowing who Paul is matters to Titus,
and he must have felt his chest swell when this letter was
opened and read to him—unless he could himself read, which
would have put him in the top 10 percent. What mattered
more to him was how Paul described himself. What Paul says
about himself frames how Titus relates to Paul, his mentor.
Paul describes himself, first, as a "servant of God" (actually
"slave of God") and, second, as "an apostle of Jesus Christ"
(1:1). He expands what this powerful Old Testament–New

Testament combo, this slave-apostle (cf. Psalm 104:26, 42; James 1:1) entails. His slave-apostleship was God's calling consistent with "the faith of God's elect and their knowledge of the truth." The NIV's "to further" stretches the meaning of a simple preposition (*kata*) in a good direction, but I back off the precision to translate it with "consistent with." The faith and knowledge of God's elect are themselves consistent with "godliness," or civilized piety (all in 1:1). Again, if you remember from our study of 1 and 2 Timothy, Paul's favorite word in these letters is *eusebeia*, which matches a common Latin word, *pietas*, and the words describe the public religious behavior of adults whose lives and witness are socially respectable. That is, these Christians possess a civilized piety in the public square, this time in Crete, that will promote human flourishing and the common good—if they live this way, the Christians will be safe (mostly).

Paul continues to define his relationship with Titus by saying he's a slave-apostle also of "the hope of eternal life" that God "promised before the beginning of time"—and the launching of that promised eternal life occurs "through the preaching" of the gospel that Paul has been "entrusted" with (1:3). Heaven, or the kingdom of God where human life will flourish as designed by God, will happen because God has promised it (McKnight, *The Heaven Promise*).

LEADERS BEGIN WELL BY AFFIRMING THEIR CHILDREN

Paul calls Titus "my true son," and here again Paul does not use the common term for "son" but the term for "child" (*teknon*, not *huios*; see 1 Timothy 1:2, 18; 2 Timothy 1:2; 2:1; and Titus 1:4). This is Paul's term especially for those he has led to Christ and even more for those he mentors so they can flourish in their gifting. The term is as endearing as much as it is a term of formation. His claim to be the father and Titus the son, however, is immediately knocked into shape with "in our common faith" (Titus 1:4). This special kind of spiritual father-son relationship is possible only in their shared, common faith.

LEADERS BEGIN WELL BY PRAYING FOR THEIR CHILDREN

The way to begin a letter is not to light up the first line with accusations and warnings and protestations. No, the polite manner of a letter opening is to provide a prayer that is read aloud in the person's presence: "Grace and peace from God the Father and Christ Jesus our Savior" to you, my dear child, Titus (1:4). Before he launches into instructions, he prays for the man. Before he prays for the man, he identifies himself and he identifies Titus, and thereby names their spiritual relationship. All this prepares for the prayer and then the instructions.

QUESTIONS FOR REFLECTION AND APPLICATION

1. What might be some good signs that a leader is prioritizing their relationships?

2. How does Paul see himself in a parental role with the people he mentors?

3. What do you think of the idea that Titus and other letter recipients may not have read their own letters, but rather had someone else read to them?

4. Have you had a parent-child relationship with someone in a spiritual context (with you either as the parent or the child)? What was that experience like?

5. Think of someone you care for or mentor. Write a short greeting-wish-prayer for them in the style of Paul's letter openings. Consider sending it to them.

FOR FURTHER READING

McKnight, Scot. *The Heaven Promise: Engaging the Bible's Truth about Life to Come.* Colorado Springs: WaterBrook, 2015.

LEADERS NEED
MATURITY

Titus 1:5–9

[5] *The reason I left you in Crete was that you might put in order what was left unfinished and appoint elders in every town, as I directed you. [6] An elder must be blameless, faithful to his wife, a man whose children believe and are not open to the charge of being wild and disobedient. [7] Since an overseer manages God's household, he must be blameless—not overbearing, not quick-tempered, not given to drunkenness, not violent, not pursuing dishonest gain. [8] Rather, he must be hospitable, one who loves what is good, who is self-controlled, upright, holy and disciplined. [9] He must hold firmly to the trustworthy message as it has been taught, so that he can encourage others by sound doctrine and refute those who oppose it.*

Paul learned quickly in his mission work to appoint leaders who could hold the tiller. Someone would eventually take hold, so qualities for the reliable pilots emerged into instructions for each house church. Paul was in Crete, and when he left, he instructed Titus to "put in order what was left unfinished" (1:5). This could suggest Paul had to leave quickly or, more likely, he was so confident in Titus's wisdom that he handed two tasks over to him (and probably many more!): to straighten things out and to "appoint elders in every town" where a house church had formed.

OVERSEERS

The New Testament uses two terms for what appears to be the highest level of leadership, the terms "elder" and "bishop" (or overseer). Twice Paul sketches the character traits for this kind of leader, once in 1 Timothy 3:1–7 (see pp. 51–52) and again in today's passage. In the former passage he called them "overseers" but here "elders." But he does use the term "elder" in the first letter as well (5:17, 19 and perhaps also 5:1). So maybe elder and overseer are the same type of leader, which becomes virtually certain in Titus, for in verse 7 he slides from "elder" to "overseer." Because the substance of this passage is much like the passage in 1 Timothy 3, I will grab a couple of sections from the study guide there and adjust them to what Paul tells Titus. But I will not discuss again the comparison with Aristotle, so I suggest you page back and read that discussion there (pp. 50–53).

OBSERVATIONS

Three observations. First, Paul's lists in Titus and in 1 Timothy 3 are not identical because his lists were not skills or a job description. He wasn't thinking of a required checklist of qualifications. The virtues he mentions *indicate a person's Christian character and maturity in discipleship.* Because the lists aren't the same in the two different letters, and the letters were written probably at about the same time, we should avoid adding them up into a master list or reducing them to common denominators. Instead, we need to perceive them as indicators of character. Overall, a leader should be a "good character" or "mature Christian" or a "committed disciple of Jesus."

Second, leadership, whether we use the term bishop, elder, or pastor, is complicated. The people in one's church will more or less shape the tasks of the leader, while the fundamental gifting and vision of the leader will in turn shape the church. So just as the moralists and philosophers of that day knew what was needed to lead a city, so Paul lists those traits he had learned were needed to lead house churches in the Roman Empire in the first century. These are experienced-based virtues for leadership in a church (small or large). Centuries have changed the experiences, and the traits needed for pastoral leadership have adjusted into all their many varieties today. After all, who has a church ministry today without a worship leader and musicians and vocalists? And most churches to this day believe pastors need seminary or at least some theological training. Those traits are at best either invisible or barely visible in Paul's lists.

But this needs to be said because it's an ignored, stinky elephant in the room. Many churches have created new boards or committees that have morphed away from the elder-overseer-pastor qualities to business and leadership and governance models. In some cases those on the newer boards are not even remotely qualified to pastor or oversee a church spiritually. In which case, to the degree that model is shaping the church, that church is eroding its essential calling to be a church. When we turn a church into a business, an organization, or an institution, we cease being the body of Christ. If you would like to read the story of one pastor who experienced the shift from the spiritual maturation model into the business model, try reading *The Pastor: A Memoir* by Eugene Peterson.

Third, I now reduce Paul's list of more than a dozen categories to six, with the terms in Titus following.

- Socially respectable: blameless
- Faithful in one's marriage and family: faithful to one's wife, believing children
- Self-controlled: relationally, socially, in drinking, physically, with money, disciplined
- Hospitable
- Teachable and teaching: hold firmly to the trustworthy message, sound doctrine, refute opponents of the gospel
- Discipled or mature: loves what is good, upright, holy

A noticeable theme in the Pastoral Epistles is the theme of civilized piety or a socially respectable life, and one theme running through all the terms he mentions in today's passage forms into "civilized piety." Paul learned from experience that church leaders do best when they behave. Jews learned how to live socially respectable lives in the Diaspora. The theme of a socially respectable life deserves more attention in churches today. A socially respectable life is earned over time when others observe character, wisdom, social conscience, justice, and fair-mindedness (McKnight, "*Eusebeia*"). The witness of a local church is most hurt by greedy leaders, abusive pastors, socially unengaged elders—in other words, the development of a bad or selfish or self-centered reputation.

But *socially* respectable is not all Paul cares about. Paul's virtues shift the focus from the public forum to house churches where Christian virtue can flourish and be practiced without reservation and with community-forming power. Each of these character traits receives a re-formation in the Jewish and Christian tradition. The primary social location for these traits is not the public forum but the house church, though the forum ought to be able to observe these traits too. Instead, the house church becomes the schoolroom in which new believers are mentored into Christian character, and virtuous people carry their virtues into the public forum, where they become socially respectable.

WOMEN LEADERS

Three points. First, Paul does not *demand* that only men can be elders or overseers. Nor does he *instruct* Titus (or Timothy) to appoint only men. Read those previous sentences twice if you have to because this idea needs emphasis. There is no statement in these lists that says, "Appoint only men." Not once does Paul say that. But second, Paul *assumes* men when he trots through his two lists. He assumes men because in most of his churches, at least for the early seasons of the house church, men would have been the leaders. Third, in 1 Timothy 3:8–10, 12–13, he assumes deacons are men , *but we know a woman deacon by name* (Phoebe; Romans 16:1–2). If Paul can assume men but know that some deacons were women, then we must exercise extreme caution in inferring from the assumption of men in the elder-overseer lists to the necessity of such leaders being men. And there were women leaders exercising significant gifts in the Pauline churches, like Nympha in Colossians 4:15 and Priscilla in Romans 16:3. Junia was an apostle (Romans 16:7), and Philip had daughters, four of them, who were prophets (Acts 21:9). If apostle and prophet were the highest of gifts, one is not unwise to think gifted women could be elders, overseers, and pastors. A major obstacle for all women of the first century was that they were much less likely to be educated when compared with men. Which is why Paul advocates for women sitting down, listening, and learning in 1 Timothy 2:11.

One final observation about women leaders in the church. The major theme of 1 Timothy especially, but resonating throughout all three of these pastoral epistles, is civilized piety, and as we have said, this term expresses a socially respectable life that can bring honor to the Lord and his gospel, as well as keep the church out of trouble. (As long as it doesn't lead to denying or watering down the gospel.) Times change, and what is civilized will shift from century to century and context to context. I want to make a strong claim that denying women giftedness and calling brings disrespect to Jesus and to the church and that silencing women hurts the witness because it is so socially disrespectable. Of course, like you, I have friends and fellow church members who don't believe in women as church leaders, who think believing such diminishes Paul's words, and who would counter that being socially respectable does not matter. I disagree. (I have sketched my view in *The Blue Parakeet*.)

QUESTIONS FOR REFLECTION AND APPLICATION

1. What does Paul delegate to Titus?

2. How do the people of a certain church shape the tasks of the leaders of that church?

3. How does using a business leadership model to choose leaders compromise the spiritual health of a church?

4. Look up the following verses where we translate with "civilized piety" or "socially respectable life," and which is traditionally translated with "godliness": 1 Timothy 2:2; 3:16; 4:7; 6:3, 6, 11; 2 Timothy 3:5; Titus 1:1. What are the topics that evoke Paul's use of this term?

5. How does this lesson impact your understanding of women in church leadership?

FOR FURTHER READING

McKnight, Scot. *The Blue Parakeet: Rethinking How You Read the Bible.* 2nd ed. Grand Rapids: Zondervan, 2018.

———. "*Eusebeia* as Social Respectability: The Public Life of the Christian Pastor." Pages 157–74 in *Rhetoric, History, and Theology: Interpreting the New Testament.* Edited by Todd D. Still and Jason A. Meyers. Lanham, MD: Lexington/Fortress Academic, 2021.

Peterson, Eugene. *The Pastor: A Memoir.* New York: HarperOne, 2011.

LEADERS FACE PROBLEM PEOPLE

Titus 1:10–16

[10] *For there are many rebellious people, full of meaningless talk and deception, especially those of the circumcision group.* [11] *They must be silenced, because they are disrupting whole households by teaching things they ought not to teach—and that for the sake of dishonest gain.* [12] *One of Crete's own prophets has said it: "Cretans are always liars, evil brutes, lazy gluttons."* [13] *This saying is true. Therefore rebuke them sharply, so that they will be sound in the faith* [14] *and will pay no attention to Jewish myths or to the merely human commands of those who reject the truth.* [15] *To the pure, all things are pure, but to those who are corrupted and do not believe, nothing is pure. In fact, both their minds and consciences are corrupted.* [16] *They claim to know God, but by their actions they deny him. They are detestable, disobedient and unfit for doing anything good.*

I don't know where, but I read in a novel about a pastor whose preferred time to go to church was when no one was there. Early morning was his favorite time. A church without messy people would be a respite for many church leaders, but such a church seems not to exist. The reality is that the church is about people, that people are the lifeblood of the church, and that people are also the problem in churches. Pastor John Burke once wrote a book with a title that summed up the message of the book and the reality of the church and its people whom he serves: *No Perfect People Allowed.*

We can agree that there are no perfect people in the church, but we affirm as well that some imperfections, in character and beliefs, have the potential to corrupt the church. Those with theological skills have more capacity to spot the problem, then mentor such people back into spiritual health, but Paul does not permit them to stay put on the skill of detection.

LEADERS NAME SERIOUS CORRUPTIONS

Some theological differences are just that: differences. At times they are little more than preferences. John Wesley, the great Reformer of England and America, once said,

> Condemn no man for not thinking as you think. Let every one enjoy the full and free liberty of thinking for himself. Let every man use his own judgment, since every man must give an account of himself to God. Abhor every approach, in any kind or degree, to the spirit of persecution, if you cannot reason nor persuade a man into the truth, never attempt to force a man into it. If love will not compel him to come, leave him to God, the judge of all. (Wesley, *Advice to the People Called Methodists*, 10)

I like what he says here because it recognizes that none of us knows the truth with perfection. But John Wesley did not create a believe-what-you-want culture either. At times someone crosses over the line of gospel truth and orthodox belief. For them, we must admit, they may be defending what they think is the truth, and you think they are denying the truth.

In cases where the truth of the gospel has been overtly denied, Paul tosses arrows aflame with fire. He calls them "rebellious people, full of meaningless talk and deception," and he knows one faction in this group of rebels is "the circumcision group" (1:10). Paul opened his mission in new cities at the synagogue, with some believing the message about Jesus as Messiah and others not believing. His persistence seems always to have led to opposition by some synagogue leaders because Paul didn't require gentile converts to follow the law. Another development occurred that spurs what he says here. Some converts to Jesus did believe Jewish and gentile believers were to follow the law of Moses as they did, which included the necessity of circumcision. At times this group gained followers and opposed Paul—and Paul warns Titus to keep his eye on this group.

In fact, he was to more than keep his eye on them. Paul says, "They must be silenced," and his term could be paraphrased with "put a plug in their mouth" (1:11). The reasons he wants their corruptions stopped is because they are infecting entire house churches with their beliefs, and they are doing it for money (1:11). He tosses a slur at them when he quotes "one of Crete's own prophets" (1:12), and then he labels their errors with eight more terms: (1) they believe in "Jewish myths," (2) they are committed to "merely human commands," (3) they "reject the truth," (4) they are "corrupted," (5) they "do not believe" the truth of the gospel, (6) their corruptions are in "both their minds and consciences," (7) "they claim to know God, but by their actions they deny him," and (8) so are "detestable, disobedient and unfit for doing anything good" (1:14–16).

About a generation ago Christian leaders began a slow learning curve of not talking like this, but this kind of vituperative language has been part of public discourse and Christian polemics for nearly two millennia. Some of the strongest language I have read like this comes from Martin Luther and John Calvin. It's hard for me to say this, but some of their language is plain hateful. Our progress into learning better how to express our deep disagreements encourages many of us. I know it does me. While Paul's language sounds like that of his contemporaries and is over the top for us, he gets at something vital for leadership.

Leaders need to name theological, behavioral, and character corruptions. Shane Claiborne has been a prophet to the greed and consumerist corruption of the American church (Claiborne, *Irresistible Revolution*). Diane Langberg has called out leaders who, corrupted by power, turn Christian cultures toxic (Langberg, *Redeeming Power*). Both do so in a Wesley-like charitableness without mincing words or entering into personal vendettas. Local leaders will discern which sins and corruptions to name, and it will be wise for them to become self-aware enough and broad-as-Wesley in not naming what others see differently. Wise leaders discern what matters most when differences slide from genuine differences into corruptions.

LEADERS AIM FOR THEIR SPIRITUAL HEALTH

Those who turn differences into vendettas block the possibility of realization of error, reformation of ideas, and restoration to the people of God. Paul urges Titus to "rebuke them sharply" but not so he can win and so the corrupted, toxic people are shamed but so "they will be sound in the faith" (1:13). The strategy of reclamation transforms how we address those who disagree with us or with whom we disagree. Why not enter into dialogue by asking questions? Not leading questions but questions shaped by genuine listening for answers for the sake of communication and dialogue. Then we can attempt to explain in their words what they believe—to their satisfaction. And only then outlining differences in a way that mentors the person toward a healthy theology. It's hard. It's often derailed by heated arguments. It's often met by stiff resistance and name-calling. Stay patient. Do it for the sake of Christ and the church, and not for personal preferences.

QUESTIONS FOR REFLECTION AND APPLICATION

1. How have you seen people be the problem in churches?

2. What is the difference between different opinions and different (nonorthodox) doctrines?

3. What were some of the people issues and difference issues that troubled Paul and his churches?

4. Which issues and types of people problems trouble your church today?

5. How can you avoid turning differences into vendettas?

FOR FURTHER READING

Burke, John. *No Perfect People Allowed: Creating a Come-as-You-Are Culture in the Church*. Grand Rapids: Zondervan, 2007.

Claiborne, Shane. *Irresistible Revolution: Living as an Ordinary Radical*. Rev. ed. Grand Rapids: Zondervan, 2016.

Langberg, Diane. *Redeeming Power: Understanding Authority and Abuse in the Church*. Grand Rapids: Brazos, 2020.

Wesley, John. *Advice to a People Called Methodists*. 1745. My thanks to Thomas Lyons for locating an original of this book, at https://play.google.com/books/reader?id=gZ9hAAAAcAAJ&pg=GBS.PA4&hl=en.

LEADERS TEACH

Titus 2:1–15

¹ [Titus]* You, however, must teach what is appropriate to sound doctrine. ² Teach the **older men** *to be temperate, worthy of respect, self-controlled, and sound in faith, in love and in endurance.*

³ Likewise, teach the **older women** *to be reverent in the way they live, not to be slanderers or addicted to much wine, but to teach what is good. ⁴ Then they can urge the younger women to love their husbands and children, ⁵ to be self-controlled and pure, to be busy at home, to be kind, and to be subject to their husbands, so that no one will malign the word of God.*

⁶ Similarly, encourage the **young men** *to be self-controlled. ⁷ [Titus] In everything set them an example by doing what is good. In your teaching show integrity, seriousness ⁸ and soundness of speech that cannot be condemned, so that those who oppose you may be ashamed because they have nothing bad to say about us.*

⁹ Teach **slaves** *to be subject to their masters in everything, to try to please them, not to talk back to them, ¹⁰ and not to steal from them, but to show that they can be fully trusted, so that in every way they will make the teaching about God our Savior attractive.*

¹¹ For the grace of God has appeared that offers salvation **to all people.** *¹² It teaches us to say "No" to ungodliness and worldly passions, and to live self-controlled, upright and godly lives in this* *present age, [13] while we wait for the blessed hope—the appearing of the glory of our great God and Savior, Jesus Christ, [14] who gave himself for us to redeem us from all wickedness and to purify for himself a people that are his very own, eager to do what is good.*

[15] *[**Titus**] These, then, are the things you should teach. Encourage and rebuke with all authority. Do not let anyone despise you.*

*Words bolded in this passage for ease of reference with what follows.

The centuries have rolled on, sometimes slowly and sometimes rapidly. At the heart of centuries rolling on are cultural changes. Here is a good example. When American men entered the military to participate in World War II, women—wives, widows, and singles—entered the workforce. Rosie the Riveter now represents the workforce of women, and the song of Ethel Merman and Ray Middleton, with the show tune by Irving Berlin, "Anything You Can Do I Can Do Better," from the Broadway musical *Annie Get Your Gun*, was their anthem. *That* women could do much of the labor men were doing is not the surprise. What surprises is that when the men came home, the women returned home— and they were none too happy about it in many cases. The stifling of the exhibited giftedness of women turned a corner in American culture. "Among married-couple families, both spouses [are] employed in 46.8 percent of families" (*Employment Characteristics of Families—2021*). What happens to the traditional mores and expectations in families when both spouses are employed? How do we live in the way of Jesus, how do we form into "godliness," or civilized piety, when our culture is so different from the culture at work in Paul's words to Titus?

Today's passage gives us an opportunity to explore those questions. We label such a passage a "household regulation" passage, and there are a few of them in the New Testament (Colossians 3:18–4:1; Ephesians 5:21–6:9; 1 Peter 2:10–3:7), not to ignore a similar kind of passage at 1 Timothy 5:1–6:2. The word "household" restricts the instructions to the various stations in life of those in a common Roman or Greek household. In today's passage Paul speaks to older men and women, to young men, to slaves, and thus to all people. And also a few times to Titus directly. I don't know why he didn't think of saying something directly to young women and instead only spoke about them to the older women, nor do I know why he didn't address fathers and mothers and children, as he did in Colossians and Ephesians. Perhaps Titus needs to address transhousehold categories that are noticeable in the house churches on Crete. Maybe the gospel mission on Crete had not yet formed singular households in which the kinds of instructions in the other Pauline letters were pertinent. What this illustrates, then, is that the gospel addresses social conditions *as they are*, not *as some kind of idealistic arrangement*. We can learn from what Paul said in his way for his day.

WHAT IS APPROPRIATE

What is "appropriate" (2:1) is our invitation to enter into the world of Titus. The word can be translated with "what is consistent" (CEB, NRSVue), or "what accords with" (ESV), or with "promote the kind of living that reflects wholesome teaching" (NLT). Each of these more or less is identical in sense: Titus is to instruct various groups of people to live in a way that corresponds to and coheres with solid theology as lived in a way that reflects the way of Jesus.

One quick glance through the New Testament alone shows the differences as the instructions of Jesus in the

Sermon on the Mount are not the same as the instructions of the apostle John in his first letter or the instructions James gave to those who would read his letter. No passage frames the core continuity with local flexibility like 1 Corinthians 9:20–23:

> To the Jews I became like a Jew, to win the Jews. To those under the law I became like one under the law (though I myself am not under the law), so as to win those under the law. To those not having the law I became like one not having the law (though I am not free from God's law but am under Christ's law), so as to win those not having the law. To the weak I became weak, to win the weak. I have become all things to all people so that by all possible means I might save some. I do all this for the sake of the gospel, that I may share in its blessings.

What is appropriate to a specific situation requires knowledge of the will of God as taught in the Bible, wisdom to discern context and what is appropriate, the Spirit's guidance that gives new creation light to the context, and a community that witnesses to the way of Jesus. The roots are in place—the ethic of Jesus, life in the Spirit, and the explicit wisdom of the letters of Paul.

OLDER FOLKS

The "older men" are instructed to live in a way not that different from the elder/overseers (Titus 1:5–9) by living a moderate, respectable, self-controlled life while they maintain theological health ("sound in faith" 2:2). As well, they are to be marked by love and resilience.

What Makes a Person Old?

Solon, then, reckons the life of man by the aforesaid ten weeks of years. And Hippocrates the physician, says that there are seven ages, those of the little boy, the boy, the lad, the young man, the man, the elderly man, the old man, and that these ages are measured by multiples of seven though not in regular succession. His words are: "In man's life there are seven seasons, which they call ages, little boy, boy, lad, young man, man, elderly man, old man. He is a little boy until he reaches seven years, the time of the shedding of his teeth; a boy until he reaches puberty, i.e. up to twice seven years; a lad until his chin grows downy, i.e. up to thrice seven years; a young man until his whole body has grown, till four times seven; a man till forty-nine, till seven times seven; an elderly man till fifty-six, up to seven times eight; after that an old man." (Philo, *On the Creation of the World*, 105, LCL; Colson and Whitaker)

More lines are devoted to the older women, and the best guessed reason for this is that there were more of them! Paul uses a graphic word that says a lot: they are to be "reverent," and this word translates a double word (*hieros, prepō*). Put literally, "what is appropriate for a priest or someone sacred"! Some may experience this as asking more of the older women than the older men, while others could perceive a profound respect for the older women.

Their priestly status for Paul means they learn not to discredit others and not to be addicted to alcohol. Noticeably, as priestlike they are "to teach what is good" (2:3). Paul does not restrict their teaching what is good to younger women, though some read it that way. But he does move to their teaching of the younger women, and what they teach draws on their own experience and context: that the younger women are "to love their husbands and children" (2:4). While loving one's husband seems rather instinctual, in this context on Crete many early Christian wives were married to unbelieving husbands, so the instruction has evangelistic value (cf. 1 Peter 3:1; 1 Corinthians 7:12–16). These younger women were instructed, like the older men, to be "self-controlled" and "pure" (a temple-shaped word, like "reverent") and, with their work life connected to the household, "to be busy at home" (2:5). The NIV here harbors potentially mistaken ideas. This text does not say "stay home," but instead it urges women to work the household well, for they, not their husbands, managed the household. The younger women then were to be good managers of the household by not abandoning the home to move from one social event to another (1 Timothy 5:13). To avoid discrediting the gospel, they are to live a socially respectable kind of Christian life in being "kind" and "subject to their husbands" (Titus 2:5).

While these terms stimulate similarities in our world, we can easily discern the basics: good women, good workers, good reputation—these are the foundation stones for Paul's instructions.

YOUNGER FOLKS

Paul does not address the younger women directly. Instead, they are addressed indirectly by his instructing the older women what to teach the younger women. Oddly, Paul has next to nothing for the younger men—he tells them "to be self-controlled" (2:6)—and this is because probably more younger women were part of the church He said much the same to the older men (2:2) and to the younger women (2:5).

That this concept appears for three different groups reveals its importance for how Paul thought Christians ought to live on Crete in the Roman Empire. It is a variant, then, on his more favorite term in the Pastoral Letters, "godliness," or civilized piety. The ethical sense is that the believers are to be moderate in lifestyle: not extravagant, not grandiose, not seeking to be seen or to be heard or to be at the top of the heap, not to be great or famous or a celebrity. Instead, they are to be good, to be godly, and to be loving.

SLAVES

Please read what I wrote about slaves at 1 Timothy 6:1–2 (pp. 80–81).

Paul and Titus did not perceive slavery of a human to another human as immoral, and that illustrates the importance of recognizing that cultures not only change but they can morally progress. What we think today about, say, money or war or how we insure ourselves or what jobs we do, may be seen as profoundly immoral in a century or two. So we can give Paul and Titus slack while we limit the specifics of this section (Titus 2:9–10). He tells them to be good slaves by working hard and being affable and agreeable, as he also tells them not to do what was well known about slaves in that day: "not to steal" (2:10). Instead, they are to be allegiant and trustworthy, and here's why: as believers, these slaves have the potential to "make the teaching about God our Savior attractive" (2:10).

ALL PEOPLE

At some level, Paul's listing of various groups promoted the idea in his head that he was talking to everyone. It's easy to like people like us and difficult to like people unlike us.

The leader is called to like all and to mentor all into the faith. Easier said than done. Leaders are to mentor all who are present, not be present only with those they like. The reason why leaders need to develop a pastoral skill for all people is because "God has appeared" in the Lord Jesus Christ—that is, God is incarnate. That manifestation "offers salvation to all people" (2:11). The NIV's addition of the word "offers" narrows what Paul actually wrote. I translate literally: "For God's grace has appeared, deliverance for all humans" or "for the deliverance for all humans."

Paul does not, like many today, get lost in an unending and unknowable debate about how many will be saved in the end. Instead, he gets lost in the glories of God's gracious redemption, a redemptive power at work in us that leads us to "say 'No' to ungodliness [or "uncivilized piety" or to "nonrespectable religion"] and worldly passions" (2:12). The redemptive power teaches us to say yes to—wait for it—to be "self-controlled" and to live "upright" and "godly" (civilized piety) lives as we await the second coming of Jesus (2:13).

In summary, the fundamentals of the transformed life, then, are saying no to sin and the world and yes to goodness and godliness—that is, to the way of Jesus—and to do this yes in a manner that promotes a good reputation for Jesus, the gospel, and the church.

AND TITUS TOO

What Paul says to Titus is what Paul would say to any leaders today. Teach these fundamentals (2:1, 7, 15) and live in a way that embodies (2:7–8) the previous summary of the fundamentals. If Titus lives like this, the church will be seen on Crete as a civilized piety.

QUESTIONS FOR REFLECTION
AND APPLICATION

1. How does the "household regulation" passage in Titus differ from similar passages in other epistles? (See Colossians 3:18–4:1; Ephesians 5:21–6:9; 1 Timothy 5:1–6:2; 1 Peter 2:10–3:7)

2. How does Paul determine appropriate advice for the widely different situations into which he writes?

3. Why might Paul have given more instructions to women than men here?

4. Why doesn't Paul address slavery more clearly in his letters?

5. What are some fruits of a transformed life that are evident in you?

FOR FURTHER READING

Bureau of Labor Statistics. *Employment Characteristics of Families—2021.* April 20, 2022. https://www.bls.gov/news.release/pdf/famee.pdf.

LEADERS DO GOOD

Titus 3:1–11

[1] *Remind the people to be subject to rulers and authorities, to be obedient, to be ready to do whatever is good,* [2] *to slander no one, to be peaceable and considerate, and always to be gentle toward everyone.*

[3] *At one time we too were foolish, disobedient, deceived and enslaved by all kinds of passions and pleasures. We lived in malice and envy, being hated and hating one another.* [4] *But when the kindness and love of God our Savior appeared,* [5] *he saved us, not because of righteous things we had done, but because of his mercy. He saved us through the washing of rebirth and renewal by the Holy Spirit,* [6] *whom he poured out on us generously through Jesus Christ our Savior,* [7] *so that, having been justified by his grace, we might become heirs having the hope of eternal life.* [8] *This is a trustworthy saying. And I want you to stress these things, so that those who have trusted in God may be careful to devote themselves to doing what is good. These things are excellent and profitable for everyone.*

[9] *But avoid foolish controversies and genealogies and arguments and quarrels about the law, because these are unprofitable and useless.* [10] *Warn a divisive person once, and then warn them a second time. After that, have nothing to do with them.* [11] *You may be sure that such people are warped and sinful; they are self-condemned.*

The word "good" (*agathos*) appears ten times in the Pastoral Letters, but its near equivalent, "excellent" or "beautiful" (*kalos*), appears twenty-one times. The concept of doing what is good emerges as a major indicator of Christian maturity in these letters. In our context, then, doing good embodies what it means to be "godly," or have civilized piety. A socially respectable religion is one in which its participants work for the common good of the community. All this to say that "good works" in the Pauline letters points to what we today call compassion ministries and social justice.

My favorite example of doing good is when Peter describes the mission and ministry of Jesus to a gentile named Cornelius. He describes Jesus to him by saying he "went around doing good" (Acts 10:38), and here the Greek word combines "good" with "working" or "doing" (*euergeteō*). In Paul's letters it works like this: God saves a human, and the Spirit empowers the human (as it did Jesus in that same verse in Acts 10) to do good works for the common good.

Leaders are to lead in doing good works and in motivating others to join them in their efforts to witness to the gospel about Jesus in a tangible, material way. In today's passage I want to shape our reflection on three kinds of "doing good": public, redemptive, and conversational.

PUBLIC GOOD

To "be subject to rulers and authorities" and "to be obedient" is best embodied in being "ready to do whatever is good" (3:1). The "whatever" is the secret sauce because the leader prepares others to do good with every opportunity they get, like someone in our church who gave a sizable donation to pave the parking lot, and a mother of schoolchildren in our church who organizes an annual gift to the local grade school

185

of backpacks, school supplies, and winter clothing. We are not to devalue these gifts because they are material or social. They are valued because we, as Jesus people, respond to those in our world in "whatever" way we can because as Jesus did good, so we too are to do good. The good doers in a community are the least likely to be slandering and the most likely to love peace and gentleness (3:2). In my decades of church life and teaching leaders in the church, those churches most committed from the heart out are those who strive as well for good relations in the community.

REDEMPTIVE GOOD

Titus 3:3–8 tells the story of Christian conversion and transformation from one way of life to a new way of life, with the new life being a life of redemptive goodness. The critical expressions are found at 3:3 and 3:4: "At one time" and "But when." The BC days (before Christ) and the AC days (after Christ).

Paul piles on the terms for the BC days: "foolish" and "disobedient" and "deceived" and "enslaved by all kinds of passions and pleasures" and "malice" and "envy" and "being hated and hating one another" (3:3). These are stereotypes of a pagan past, and one way to tell the story is to exaggerate the bad and ignore all the good so the new days with Christ shine forth in all their newness. I've read or heard a thousand such exaggerated tales of conversion, and that they are "tale" is not so much a criticism as it is the way many learn to tell their story to magnify the goodness of God.

Who makes us good? Our Savior-God's "kindness and love" then "appeared" (3:4) in our lives and God "saved us" (3:5). But he did not save us on the basis of our righteous works but on the basis of his "mercy" (3:5). Salvation and baptism, once we get used to how the New Testament talks about them, form a unity in the early church. If you asked someone when they were saved, they more than likely would say, "I got baptized last autumn," or something like that. Paul says much the same here when he writes that God "saved us [1] through the washing of rebirth and renewal by the Holy Spirit, whom he poured out on us generously [2] through Jesus Christ our Savior, so that, having been [3] justified by his grace, we might become [4] heirs having the hope of eternal life" (3:5–7, numbers added). Notice the four elements at work here: the baptism by water embodies a cleansing operation of the Holy Spirit that brings a new life, and this happens only by what Jesus has done in his death and resurrection and ascension, and that work by Jesus makes us right with God so that we have hope with all those who are in God's family.

Those are elements of our redemption, and the redeemed "devote themselves to doing what is good" (3:8). I call this the "redemptive good" of the redeemed. When Paul then closes this paragraph, he refers to "these things," and they are the elements of redemption that lead to doing good work. Ever exploring a fresh way of saying much the same, Paul sticks a label on these good works in 3:8 with two words. The first is "excellent" (*kalos*), and I like to translate this word with "beautiful," as it is an aesthetic judgment about the quality of good works. The second is "profitable," the same word used for the Bible at 2 Timothy 3:16—and these two descriptors of good works are for humans (the NIV has "everyone"). On Paul's mind is that our behaviors are observed by God and also by humans—and for Titus, the general population on Crete.

CONVERSATIONAL GOOD

A leader committed to doing good for the common good and living a life of good works rooted in redemption in Christ will develop the skill of avoiding conversational toxicities while forming a life of conversational good. To check yourself, check your Twitter. A leader I know once said, "When I'm angry, I get on Twitter. Otherwise, I hang out on Instagram and sometimes Facebook." Paul must know what Twitter is all about when he says "avoid foolish controversies" (3:9), but he takes us back to his most common setting for strife: his fellow Jews who either disbelieve Jesus is the Messiah or his fellow Jewish believers who think there should be more law for the gentiles. So he adds avoid "genealogies and arguments and quarrels about the law" because they are "unprofitable and useless" (3:9). One could translate them "unuseful and useless," as I do in *The Second Testament*.

So, to form a conversationally good life, the leader needs to get away from, or avoid or warn, divisive people in the community or church, and he limits the times. Do that once or twice and then move on. His image is to stay away from such chatterings. Such people, he tells Titus, are not the redeemed out for doing good—someday, perhaps, they will be.

Mark in your community people who do good, and watch them. They will contribute to the common good, they will be prompted to do good by redemption, and they will show you how to engage with those looking for a verbal tussle.

QUESTIONS FOR REFLECTION AND APPLICATION

1. How could we understand Paul's use of "good works" in today's terms?

2. Look up the idea of good at 1 Timothy 1:5, 19; 2:10; 5:10; 2 Timothy 2:21; 3:17; Titus 1:16; 2:5, 10; 3:1. Another word like good is "excellent, beautiful" [*kalos*], and it appears twenty-one times in these same letters: 1 Timothy 1:8, 18; 2:3; 3:1, 7, 13; 4:4, 6; 5:10, 25; 6:12, 13, 18, 19; 2 Timothy 1:14; 2:3; 4:7; Titus 2:7, 14; 3:8, 14. What in the context would be the "good works" that a person would be doing?

3. What does Paul consider "public good" work?

4. What is the difference between conversational toxicity and conversational good?

5. Do a social media audit on yourself. Are you conversing in "good" ways?

LEADERS ADMINISTRATE THE GOSPEL MISSION

Titus 3:12–15

¹² *As soon as I send Artemas or Tychicus to you, do your best to come to me at Nicopolis, because I have decided to winter there.* ¹³ *Do everything you can to help Zenas the lawyer and Apollos on their way and see that they have everything they need.* ¹⁴ *Our people must learn to devote themselves to doing what is good, in order to provide for urgent needs and not live unproductive lives.*

¹⁵ *Everyone with me sends you greetings. Greet those who love us in the faith.*

Grace be with you all.

One more time we come to the end of a letter by Paul only to discover some more names of his close fellow workers in the gospel mission. Here we meet Artemas and Tychicus and Zenas and Apollos. It appears Paul is sending to Crete four gospel agents. When they arrive, Paul wants Titus to come join him in Nicopolis (western Greece). The first two will take over for Titus, while the second two are to be sent on to other mission works. At some date Titus will do mission work in Dalmatia (2 Timothy 4:10). Leaders administrate when they do their work with excellence.

Leaders will instruct people in the church to do what is "good," though this time the word is *kalos*, so I suggest "excellent" or "beautiful," and in this context the beautiful work is to provide for mission agents in their mission work, whether it is the first two staying in Crete or the second two moving on to another location.

The network is tight: the believers in Nicopolis know a unity with the believers on Crete, and so they send on greetings through Paul, who sends them through these four mission agents. And Paul wants them in turn to greet those in Crete, and with his customary stroke of Christian theology, wishes God's grace on all of them (3:15).

QUESTIONS FOR REFLECTION AND APPLICATION

1. What are your key takeaways from Paul's letter to Titus?

2. What do you imagine are some of the similarities and differences between Timothy and Titus?

3. Why does Paul use such strong and colorful language about people from Crete?

4. What do you observe about Paul as a leader in this letter?

5. What do you plan to change or grow in as a result of studying the epistle to Titus?

PHILEMON

LEADERS WELCOME COMMUNICATIONS

Philemon 1–3

¹ Paul, a prisoner of Christ Jesus, and Timothy our brother,

To Philemon our dear friend and fellow worker— ² also to Apphia our sister and Archippus our fellow soldier—and to the church that meets in your home:

³ Grace and peace to you from God our Father and the Lord Jesus Christ.

Perhaps the first item noticed by Philemon, the leader of a house church in Colossae, was Paul's good manners. Emails tend not to have a greeting, and if they do, the greeting is usually brief and informal ("How ya doin'?"). The emails I write and those I receive jump immediately into the subject at hand. We have forgotten the customary manners of ancient letter writing. Our letters tend to be more like turning to the next person at a dinner conversation than the rare personal communication that ancient letters were. Think of the cost and time it took for a letter to be written, revised, and then professionally inscribed, sealed, and given to a courier, who then traveled from the place of writing, which I think was

Ephesus, to Colossae—a three- to four-day walking trip. So a letter arriving at the front door was a red-letter day.

KNOWING THE WRITERS

Paul's letter is arranged as people were taught to write such letters, beginning with the sender (1a), the addressee (1b–2), and a greeting. The letter is not scraps written on some broken piece of pottery but formal. Philemon, Apphia, and Archippus, who knew Paul and Timothy, would have observed the good manners of the letter's opening. This was two sages sending a proper letter. They would also have empathized with Paul because he was in prison, and they would have appreciated family relations with Timothy, who was also a brother to all three addressees. As they listened to the letter read aloud, they heard the reading in the voices of their sages.

HEARING THEIR NAMES

Leaders deserve to be recognized for who they are and what they do in a community of faith. The chests of Philemon, Apphia, and Archippus surely swelled that the apostle Paul himself, along with his "bestie," had chosen to write them a letter. They heard their names read aloud to open this letter. At this point they didn't know why Paul and his associates wrote this letter, so their chests were on full swell. Paul and Timothy's pin would pop it soon enough, but at this point good manners obtain. In front of the whole church, the chest-swellers heard that Philemon was "our dear friend" (or, better yet, "the one we love"), that Apphia was a sibling (or, just "sister Apphia"), and that Archippus was "our fellow soldier" (1–2). The sages, Paul and Timothy, knew their names. The others in the church heard these affirming words and surely looked at the three locals when their names were mentioned.

Who are these three? We don't know much about either Apphia or Archippus. Apphia, like Phoebe (Romans 16:1), is a sister in Christ. We don't know if she was married to Philemon, the mother of Archippus, or a leader in the church with her husband (cf. Romans 16:3–4, 7). We don't know much about Archippus either. Like Epaphroditus, he was a fellow soldier (Philippians 2:25), but we do learn that he participated in the Pauline gospel mission to gentiles (Colossians 4:17). Maybe these were three house church leaders or pastors. We don't know. (And it's OK not to know what can't be known.)

We do know a little more about Philemon: Paul and Timothy love him (1), he's a co-worker in the mission (1), the church meets in his home (2), he's a slaveowner with the power to do what he wants to Onesimus, his slave; and Paul offers restitution to Philemon for any losses (18–19), Paul plans to visit him (22), and in the end the decision of what to do to Onesimus upon his return is in Philemon's hands.

ACCEPTING THE GREETING

The good manners of an ancient letter opened as well with a greeting (3). This letter's opening greeting turns on a Christian lathe the customary Greek or Roman letter's greeting and fashions it with Christian sensibilities: "Grace and peace" may be Greek or Roman, but for a Christian they evoke the love of God and the peace God makes with humans through Christ and the Spirit to form Christians marked by gracious responses to one another and peaceful relations.

Social manners, like the formal words in this letter's greeting, in our day at times sound like a sales job more than genuine manners, but good manners are always good.

If the three addressees themselves had good manners, they would have responded quietly to themselves or even aloud, "And grace and peace to you, Paul and Timothy." Good manners matter. Edith Wharton, in her classic novel *The Age of Innocence*, with more than a little wit and satire, once wrote that "Old New York scrupulously observed the etiquette of hospitality, and no discussion with a guest was ever allowed to degenerate into a disagreement" (226). As we read this letter, we will have to use our imagination to wonder if Paul would have fit in "Old New York." Good manners will disagree, but it can be done in a mannerly way.

QUESTIONS FOR REFLECTION AND APPLICATION

1. What is the setting and context of Paul's letter to Philemon?

2. How does Paul show his good manners in this letter?

3. Who are the recipients of this letter, and why do they matter?

4. How does Paul create new Christian ideas out of old and existing Greek and Roman ideas? What are some examples?

5. How does this lesson help you appreciate the importance and preciousness of Paul's letters to his first recipients?

FOR FURTHER READING

Wharton, Edith. *The Age of Innocence*. New York: Knopf, 1993.

LEADERS
LISTEN

Philemon 4–7

4 I always thank my God as I remember you in my prayers, 5 because I hear about your love for all his holy people and your faith in the Lord Jesus. 6 I pray that your partnership with us in the faith may be effective in deepening your understanding of every good thing we share for the sake of Christ. 7 Your love has given me great joy and encouragement, because you, brother, have refreshed the hearts of the Lord's people.

Church leaders are called to nurture in themselves Christian virtues, and it's good for them to hear that their forming virtues are visible. For a sage to affirm other leaders requires listening to the leaders, and it also requires leaders to listen to sages. The best leaders lead by listening, and only listening leaders genuinely lead. A nursery rhyme, and no one knows its origins, still speaks (see the For Further Reading section for source):

> A wise old owl lived in an oak,
> The more he saw, the less he spoke

The less he spoke, the more he heard,
Now, wasn't he a wise old bird?

In public settings, listening sages in the church can affirm the virtues of other listening leaders in the church.

What the sages of this letter heard in their listening was the virtuous character of the leaders of the house churches in Colossae. At the top of the list of Christian virtues is love because it was embodied and taught by Jesus (Mark 12:28–34), and because Paul himself had settled on love as the supreme fruit of the Spirit (Galatians 5:22), the epitome of virtue (1 Corinthians 13), and the unifier in the church (Colossians 3:14). Right next to love stood the virtue of faith in three senses: (1) for the singular, especially initial, act of trusting in Jesus Christ as the agent of redemption; (2) for the ongoing life of trust in the sense of allegiance to king Jesus as Lord; and (3) for the content of what one believes about Christ (The Faith, as in the later Nicene Creed). Philemon is known for both his love and his faithfulness.

Paul is about to affirm Philemon's virtues publicly, and Philemon is about to listen to Paul's affirmations.

LISTENING FOR LOVE

Paul, now speaking for both Timothy and himself in saying "I," thanks God for Philemon's, now representing all three addressees, love and faith. (From this point on I will only occasionally remind us of the dual authors and the triple receivers of this letter.) Philemon's love is "for all his holy people" (Philemon 5). Many translations have "saints," but that term evokes for many only the very best of those who have followed Jesus—the A plusses of the Christian tradition—like Peter and Saint Francis and Macrina and Saint Teresa of Avila.

The term "holy" (*hagios*) describes the presence of God and anything designated for and devoted to God. In that sense, it's more general and applies to all those who want to follow Jesus. Philemon loves "all" those devoted to God—and this little word "all" will soon take on a very special sense.

The apostle Paul publicly affirms Philemon for having the most important virtues of the Christian faith. Leaders both affirm others and appreciate being affirmed. The fellowship of the church nurtures mutual affirmations, and leaders need these affirmations as much as anyone else, perhaps at times more because of the intense scrutiny they endure from those in the fellowship.

LISTENING FOR POTENTIAL

Particularly young and new leaders in a Christian organization or church need to hear of their potential. Philemon's "partnership" (or "fellowship"; Greek is *koinonia*) in a common allegiance to Christ has potential ("may be effective") to deepen Philemon's perception of everything that is good about this new way of life marked by love and faith in Christ (6). Paul knows Philemon is the kind of leader who can do the right thing at the right time, and he wants everyone in the assembly to hear this about Philemon.

Now, I happen to love what Paul says in verse 6 because at first reading it sounds both so very good but also so very abstract. What is perception? What is good? In this letter the perception will quickly turn into an enslaved man named Onesimus and what is good will become welcoming him back into the household of Philemon. One could point fingers at Paul for leading Philemon into a corner. Instead, Paul is being diplomatic by setting the stage for an "ask" that is soon to be heard in the room as well.

LISTENING FOR ENCOURAGEMENT

Paul having set the stage, verse 7 now takes on a sharper profile. Paul now publicly affirms how Philemon has been, like Barnabas (Acts 4:36), an encourager of others. Paul affirms this of Philemon in three ways: first, he publicly affirms how Philemon's love has become a fountain of joy for Paul; second, that same love has been an encouragement to Paul; and third, Philemon's love for others means his "empathies have come to rest on the devoted ones through you." The NIV's translation is quite different from what I have just offered. The NIV reads "because you, brother, have refreshed the hearts of the Lord's people" (7). The NIV's "hearts" translates not the normal word for heart (*kardia*) but another Greek term, *splangchna*, which refers to one's inner organs that are moved by compassion into an action to relieve someone's pain or suffering.

Again, Philemon (as well as Apphia and Archippus) publicly hear affirmations from their two sages about the formation of Christian virtues in their lives. In this letter Paul will base a plea for Philemon to welcome Onesimus back because of Philemon's virtues of love, faith, and empathy.

QUESTIONS FOR REFLECTION AND APPLICATION

1. Why does Paul consider love to be the premier virtue and fruit?

2. What does holy mean to Paul?

3. Why and how does Paul affirm Philemon in this letter?

4. Why do you think Paul talks about the guts instead of the heart here?

5. How might you be feeling at this point in the letter if you were Philemon?

FOR FURTHER READING

Wikipedia. s.v. "A Wise Old Owl." Last modified August 12, 2022. https://en.wikipedia.org/wiki/A_Wise_Old_Owl.

LEADERS FEEL

Philemon 8–11

[8] *Therefore, although in Christ I could be bold and order you to do what you ought to do,* [9] *yet I prefer to appeal to you on the basis of love. It is as none other than Paul—an old man and now also a prisoner of Christ Jesus—* [10] *that I appeal to you for my son Onesimus, who became my son while I was in chains.* [11] *Formerly he was useless to you, but now he has become useful both to you and to me.*

God expresses nothing less than godly feelings. David Lamb has recently written about seven of God's emotions: yes, hatred and wrath, along with jealousy, sorrow, joy, compassion, and love. Each of these terms could be given various translations, but what needs to be seen is that God is not distant, emotionless, unfeeling, calculating. God is a person, God has relations, God responds to us as we respond to God. That's step one. Step two is this: We are made in God's image. If Christ is the perfect image of God, and if Jesus is filled with empathies and compassions and tears and joys and love, then we too are emotional, feeling-shaped images of God. Step three: Paul's emotions and appeals to emotions come into full display in our passage.

It is not difficult for manipulative types to manufacture

feelings in others, or even to fake their own feelings, to get what they want. Their "skill" is a fraudulent art form of persuasion. But as one philosopher said, "Kitsch is fake art, expressing fake emotions, whose purpose is to deceive the consumer into thinking he feels something deep and serious, when in fact he feels nothing at all" (Scruton, *Confessions*, 9). Perceptive listeners, skilled as they are like a good antiquarian, spot the fake from the genuine. Paul was no fake artist. His feelings tripped on his tunic.

Philemon 8–11 is an emotional appeal to Philemon. And Philemon still does not know what for! Feelings are so common for Paul that he may not even realize the emotional power of this paragraph. He may not have, but Philemon did.

LEADERS FEEL RELATIONSHIPS

First, Paul appeals to his status when he says, "In Christ I could be bold and order you to do what you ought to do" (8)—again, Philemon doesn't even know yet what this order could have been. Paul degrades his own status as an apostle to motivate Philemon on the basis of a human's deepest emotion: love (9a). Let's admit something here: if you tell someone you could order them and then tell them you want them to do something on the basis of love, you've backed up your love with your order. I'll cut Paul some slack and say he wants Philemon to respond to Paul's (about to be given) ask because of their personal, emotional relationship of love. It's an appeal of "Because I love you" or "Because you love me" or "Because we love each other."

LEADERS FEEL EMPATHY

Second, he appeals to Philemon's empathy for Paul's age and imprisonment (9b). Remember, Philemon still does not know what Paul's about to ask, but he knows now that Paul loves him and that he's an aged man sitting in some confinement. He's probably in some house arrest awaiting a court appearance. Imprisonment was not a punishment in the ancient world but a temporary situation prior to a judge's decision. If you have ever seen someone unjustly confined—say the famous photo of Nelson Mandela visiting his prison cell on Robben Island—your feelings of empathy, sorrow, compassion may ignite as you read the aged Paul informing Philemon that he is a "prisoner of Christ Jesus" (9b).

LEADERS FEEL FAMILY

Third, Paul induces paternal feelings in Philemon—perhaps for Archippus—when he speaks of "my son Onesimus" (10). The name Onesimus, so common for first-century enslaved males, means "useful" but also something like "handyman." The common word for "son" is *huios*, but Paul does not use that term here. He uses *teknon*, which evokes "child" in the faith ("became my" child) and a child being mentored into leadership. The same term is used for Timothy (1 Timothy 1:2) and for those whom he led to Christ in Corinth (1 Corinthians 4:17).

Onesimus, the Slave

By all means, let us ponder again what it means to be a slave, a person enslaved. Here is one of the world's experts, Keith Bradley, defining a slave: "Slavery by definition is a means of securing and maintaining an involuntary labour force by a group in society which monopolises political and economic power" (Bradley, *Slaves and Masters*, 18).

> Slavery in the Roman world was about status and integrity and identity, all three reshaped by turning a person into a utility. Most slave were born into slavery, which means perhaps Onesimus's mother was a slave in Philemon's household. A slave's life was dependent on the master's character; good and kind masters were better than cruel ones. A male slave remained in the status of a "boy" his entire life, unless emancipated, in order to prevent a legal marriage, legal control of (their nonlegal marital relationship) children, and thus legal inheritance rights. Slaves were commonly abused physically and sexually.
>
> Onesimus was from Colossae (Colossians 4:9), he probably ran away, which was common, and he was subsequently converted to Christ through Paul (Philemon 10).

LEADERS FEEL CONVERSION

Fourth, if we tie verses 10 and 11 together, Paul also appeals to the religious, emotional experience of conversion. As Onesimus, the enslaved person who is the subject matter of this letter, became a believer through Paul while Paul was in prison, so Philemon will hear Paul's words and, as a leader, say, "I know what happened to Onesimus. It happened to me. We are alike." The conversion is powerful enough in Onesimus for Paul to play with his name as the man who was formerly use*less* but has become use*ful*.

Paul's not manipulating Philemon. Instead, he brings a fuller dimension of our personhood into the circle of persuasion. Paul respects emotions, Philemon will experience emotions as this letter is read, and they will factor into the decision Philemon is about to make. Emotionless decisions are half decisions, and "going by the book" at times will deny essential elements of what it means to be made in God's image.

My former student Becky Castle Miller is researching a dissertation on emotions in the Gospel of Luke. She wrote in a recent blog post, "Emotions are a beautiful part of the way God created us. Emotions keep us safe, help us live an abundant life, and motivate us to take action based on our values and goals. . . . Because God is emotional, and Jesus as God incarnate is emotional, it stands to reason that God not only approves of emotion but also intentionally created us as emotional beings. Our emotions are part of being made as God's image bearers" (Castle Miller, "Confusion").

QUESTIONS FOR REFLECTION AND APPLICATION

1. How does Paul use emotional appeals to Philemon?

2. What parental emotions might Paul have engendered in Philemon?

3. How do you imagine Philemon felt at this point in hearing the letter?

4. What do you think about the idea of God and Jesus being emotional?

5. How do you approach emotions in your spiritual life? What might it be like for you to become more emotional, like Paul?

FOR FURTHER READING

Bradley, Keith R. *Slaves and Masters in the Roman Empire: A Study in Social Control.* New York: Oxford University Press, 1987.

Castle Miller, Becky. "Confusion around Emotions after Spiritual Abuse." *Whole Emotion* (blog). January 9, 2023. https://beckycastlemiller .substack.com/p/confusion-around-emotions -after-spiritual. On emotions and feelings, which are not identical, I have learned much from Becky Castle Miller. Without her work I could not have written the study guide.

Lamb, David T. *The Emotions of God: Making Sense of a God Who Hates, Weeps, and Loves.* Downers Grove, IL: InterVarsity Press, 2022.

McKnight, Scot. *The Letter to Philemon.* New International Commentary on the New

Testament. Grand Rapids: Eerdmans, 2017, 6–36.

Scruton, Roger. *Confessions of a Heretic: Selected Essays*. Widworthy Barton Honiton, Devon: Notting Hill, 2016.

LEADERS DELEGATE

Philemon 12–16

¹²I am sending him—who is my very heart—back to you. ¹³I would have liked to keep him with me so that he could take your place in helping me while I am in chains for the gospel. ¹⁴But I did not want to do anything without your consent, so that any favor you do would not seem forced but would be voluntary. ¹⁵Perhaps the reason he was separated from you for a little while was that you might have him back forever— ¹⁶no longer as a slave, but better than a slave, as a dear brother. He is very dear to me but even dearer to you, both as a fellow man and as a brother in the Lord.

The single biggest temptation for Christian leaders is the abuse of power in the exercise of authority. Listen to Diane Langberg, a sage when it comes to redeeming power:

> Using theological knowledge to manipulate people to achieve our own ends is a wrong use of power.
>
> Exploiting our position in the home or the church to get our own way, serve our own ends, crush others, silence them, and frighten them is a wrong use of power.

Using our influence or our reputation to get others to further our own ends is a wrong use of power. (Langberg, *Redeeming Power*, 12)

The biggest challenge for those leaders is to lay down power, to use their power for others, to distribute their power to others. Notice what happens in this passage. It's easy to miss. Paul, the apostle, the father of gentile churches all over modern-day Turkey, sends the runaway slave Onesimus back to Philemon. Not only does he do that, he also surrenders a momentous decision to Philemon. Paul clearly hints that he would like to have Onesimus back because he's been so "useful" in the gospel work, but the decision has been delegated to Philemon. Paul could have told Philemon what to do; he could have offered his opinion without Philemon asking for it. But, instead, he sent the man back and said to Philemon, "The decision is yours." Hands off. Trusting. Delegating. Delegating redeems power.

What Happened?

The most common and ancient interpretation of Onesimus is that he was a runaway slave, was converted, and then was sent back to his slave owner, Philemon. Not all agree with this classic interpretation, which is assumed in this study guide and in my commentary on Philemon (see Introduction). Some today think Onesimus did not so much run away but "ran away" only to get Paul to become his advocate with his friend Philemon. In this case, he did not run away as a fugitive, but ran away only to get justice, in

---

which case, he planned from the beginning to return to Philemon. A few think Philemon sent Onesimus to Paul for a mission purpose and Paul sent him back, hoping Philemon would then send him back yet again to Paul on a more permanent basis.

PHILEMON KNOWS PAUL LOVES ONESIMUS

Paul, to use social media lingo, "hearted" Onesimus in public. He says of him that he is "my very heart," and again the NIV translates *splangchna* as "heart" (12). Not so. The term refers to the organs that are moved when seeing someone in pain or suffering. Maybe we can translate "the man is my own empathies" or "my feelings" or "my compassions." One can't speak of one's love for another person like this and not evoke just how much Paul loves Onesimus.

Even more, Paul informs the entire household that he would have preferred to "keep him with me" because of Onesimus's—like Philemon's—contribution to the Pauline mission to spread the gospel through the Roman Empire (13).

PHILEMON KNOWS HE MAKES THE DECISION

Philemon quickly comprehends the force of his power to make the decision—just what it is we still do not know, but it's getting clear that it's all about Onesimus. First, Philemon experiences the embodied presence of his slave because Paul is sending him back (12). In sending him back, Paul delegates the power of decision to Philemon: "I did not want to do anything without your consent" (14). The word "consent" refers to Philemon receiving the facts, weighing his options, and rendering a knowledgeable decision. Paul thickens Philemon's power when he says he wants Philemon's decision to be "voluntary" (14).

I'm impressed with Paul's self-sacrifice of his own power—he could have ordered Philemon (8). He chose not to. He chose to give Philemon the opportunity to learn how to decide about a difficult personal, Christian, and business decision on the basis of what happens to enslaved people when they convert to Christ and become—I anticipate—siblings. This must have been a constant experience in the early church.

PHILEMON KNOWS GOD'S WORK IN ONESIMUS

Paul attempts to explain what has happened in providential terms, but he does so without the arrogance of many theologians these days. "Perhaps" (15) he says, instead of "I know why God did this." Paul has a humble faith about his capacity to discern the work of God in their midst. Some people seem to think they know why everything happens and exactly what God is doing in all things. This is called "attribution theory" and refers to the need for some to attribute a reason or a motive for everything that happens. Perhaps we would do better to learn to trust God and then to speak of what we learned by faith.

Paul attributes Onesimus's conversion as what is in need of explanation. What Paul explains is that now that the man has been baptized, Philemon's got him back forever and ever (15). But something has changed, and it's dramatic: "no longer as a slave" (16)!! Surely some in the household were scratching a big "Wuuut?" graffito on a wall in Colossae. Others may have scratched "Onesimus, our brother."

God's work not only turns the man into a sibling in Christ—a child-in-the-faith whom Paul loves—but also Onesimus is now loved even more by Philemon because he can be loved doubly: in the flesh as a household member (and still a slave, probably) and as a sibling in Christ (16).

Just what this means in a Christian household is not clear, but in a letter written at nearly the same time, Colossians, here's how Paul says it. He tells the slave masters there to treat their slaves "with rightness and equality" (Colossians 4:1, my translation). The word "equality" tells the whole story. The waters of baptism wash away social inequalities and turn each person into one of two options: brother or sister. Or into one option: sibling. The result of this revolution by water became one of the biggest challenges Christian households experienced.

The transformation of Philemon's Christian household was put in the hands of Philemon, and as a leader it was his responsibility to listen to the sages (Paul and Timothy) and to lead his church into the new ways of Christ.

By the way, Paul still has not made the big ask. That's next.

QUESTIONS FOR REFLECTION
AND APPLICATION

1. How have you seen leading Christians use power wrongly?

2. How does Paul subvert power-over structures by giving Philemon a choice in returning Onesimus to Paul?

3. Why is Onesimus so precious to Paul?

4. What do you think about how the early church might have handled slaves who became fellow followers of Jesus?

5. How could "sibling" language help us navigate deep social divides between different types of Christians today?

FOR FURTHER READING

Langberg, Diane. *Redeeming Power: Understanding Authority and Abuse in the Church*. Grand Rapids: Brazos, 2020.

LEADERS DECIDE

Philemon 17–21

¹⁷ So if you consider me a partner, welcome him as you would welcome me. ¹⁸ If he has done you any wrong or owes you anything, charge it to me. ¹⁹ I, Paul, am writing this with my own hand. I will pay it back—not to mention that you owe me your very self. ²⁰ I do wish, brother, that I may have some benefit from you in the Lord; refresh my heart in Christ. ²¹ Confident of your obedience, I write to you, knowing that you will do even more than I ask.

You would not be the first person to wonder why Paul and Timothy took so long to turn on the light in the room. The long listening that occurred in the household of Philemon was how Paul prepared the entire audience for two words: "Welcome him." (The "him" being Onesimus.) The letter is quite the rhetorical presentation, and I recognize no hints of manipulation.

DECISIONS NETWORK WITH OTHERS

"If you share a common life with me" (17, my translation), Paul says, you can choose to welcome Onesimus back into the household. From the opening of this letter, Paul has forged a network of loving relations between Philemon and himself. The network flows out of being siblings in Christ, but the river is wider and stronger than even that. The network involves Philemon's coparticipation in the Pauline mission to preach the gospel to gentiles. In that network, Paul gives the ask. Onesimus ran away; Onesimus became a believer through Paul; Onesimus shined as a believer so much that Paul incorporated him into his mission; but Onesimus belongs to Philemon, not to Paul. So Paul sends him back. The "him" who is sent back is not the former "him" but a brand new "him." He's no longer a slave; he's better than a slave—he's a brother in Christ.

Philemon's welcoming of Onesimus enters both of them into a networked relationship: so close is Onesimus to Paul and Philemon to Paul that Paul claims the reception of Onesimus is a reception of Paul. There is a famous rabbinic saying that says "a person's agent is like himself" (Cohen, *The Oxford Annotated Mishnah*). Jesus said this as well when he said, "Anyone who welcomes you welcomes me, and anyone who welcomes me welcomes the one who sent me" (Matthew 10:40). Paul has simply extended the word of Jesus toward the word of the rabbis to say welcoming Onesimus is welcoming himself. Think about it: reception of others forms into a network of reception.

Paul deepens the network when he says, "If he has done you any wrong" (18). The standard explanation is that Onesimus ran away, and runaways almost always stole what they needed while on the lam. So Paul says he will pay for anything it has cost Philemon. Then Paul deepens his word by writing out—now in his own hand—an IOU in this letter to make a promissory note that he is responsible for whatever costs occurred. With a real kicker to finish off his promise: "not to mention," which Paul is about to mention, "that you owe me your very self," and this is because Philemon, too, became a believer through Paul's mission to the gentiles (19).

DECISIONS AFFIRM OTHERS

Paul goes emotional when he says, "I do wish, brother, that I may have some benefit from you in the Lord; refresh my heart in Christ" (20). The word "refresh" is the same word translated "refreshed" (7), and the word leads the listening leaders in the household to think of significant moments of emotional relief and joy and even overflowing exuberance. What Philemon senses is that his decision will directly affect the emotional well-being of his sage, the apostle Paul. Paul often informed others that his emotional state depended on the response of others to his instructions (cf. 2 Corinthians 2:12–13 and 7:2–7). When a leader like Philemon decides in congruence with his sage, Paul, a gush flows into Paul about their unity as Philemon affirms what Paul desired most: the welcoming of Onesimus. Congruent decisions form an emotional bond between leaders.

DECISIONS EXPAND

Paul now says something that has vexed us all. What did he mean when he said, "You will do even more than I ask" (21)? And did you notice that he opens this verse with the oh-so-clever "Confident of your *obedience*"? I add the italics because previously he had turned away from ordering Philemon to voluntary decision (8, 14). He puts a little pressure on Philemon here, but our concern is what did he think "even more" meant? The one option that we would all like to think is that Paul wanted him to emancipate Onesimus, and I consider that a possibility but not a likely one. What seems more likely, in keeping with his delegation of the decision to Philemon himself, is that Paul wanted Philemon to explore more deeply what happens when one of the household slaves becomes a sibling in Christ: more just treatment, more equitable and equal relationships, less harsh discipline, and most of all, a responsibility to love and trust one another because of the new life in Christ. I don't believe Paul ever saw the immorality of slavery, and few did in the ancient world. But I do believe the launching of a new creation in Christ knocked down doors and threw open windows and led to one experiment after another to live out a new way of life. Paul is saying to Philemon something like what we heard in *Hamilton*: "Don't throw away your shot, Philemon!"

Our decisions are made in a network of relationships with the possibility of rippling out from that decision to other people and other potentialities. Paul not only delegated authority to Philemon, but he handed over the decision to the man as well. What decision he made would reveal to the household and community what kingdom living looked like.

QUESTIONS FOR REFLECTION AND APPLICATION

1. How do networked relationships function in this section of the letter?

2. Analyze the rhetoric of Paul's letter and especially the argumentation of his appeal to Philemon. What do you find compelling about Paul's argument?

3. Why do you think Paul hangs his emotional state on other people's responses to his letters?

4. How do you feel about Paul not teaching people to emancipate their slaves?

5. What would you have done if you were Philemon?

FOR FURTHER READING

Cohen, Shaye J. D., Robert Goldenberg, and Hayim Lapin, eds. *The Oxford Annotated Mishnah: A New Translation of the Mishnah, with Introductions and Notes*. New York: Oxford University Press, 2022.

LEADERS MINISTER TOGETHER

Philemon 22–25

²² *And one thing more: Prepare a guest room for me, because I hope to be restored to you in answer to your prayers.*

²³ *Epaphras, my fellow prisoner in Christ Jesus, sends you greetings.* ²⁴ *And so do Mark, Aristarchus, Demas and Luke, my fellow workers.*

²⁵ *The grace of the Lord Jesus Christ be with your spirit.*

Readers tend to skim over or overtly ignore the end of Paul's letters, but there are often little morsels of reality that inform careful readers of his themes and his friends. The ending of Philemon does both.

A THEME

Think of what "Prepare a guest room for me" means when tied to the fact that Philemon has been praying for Paul to be "restored" to fellowship with him (22). Other than a few hugs and cheek-to-cheek kisses between the two, what do you think Paul did first when he got to Colossae (assuming he did)? Yes, you are right. He asked, "How's Onesimus?"

Philemon's answer will have revealed exactly how congruent his decision was with the Pauline mission and theology of oneness in Christ.

How often simple actions tell the whole story of the gospel. Hugging Onesimus told Onesimus that the gospel was effective and transformative and that he was now part of the family again. When we "perform" this letter in classes or churches, I ask whoever plays Philemon to decide what to do, and every time (so far!) he has embraced Onesimus. The classes and churches then smile and clap, and one time they stood up and gave the situation a standing ovation. Imagine how Onesimus felt. How Philemon felt. How Apphia and Archippus and other members of the household (including other slaves and servants) felt when Philemon embraced his runaway.

Some Friends

As hearing their names mattered to Philemon, Apphia, and Archippus, so now the names of others will generate past relations with some in the household of Philemon. So I provide Bible references to Paul's friends here:

Epaphras (Colossians 1:7–12; 4:12) is in prison with Paul as Paul writes this letter (Philemon 23). Mark is a gospel writer and companion of Paul (Acts 12:12, 25; 15:36–41; Colossians 4:10; 2 Timothy 4:11; and 1 Peter 5:13). Aristarchus was from Macedonia and shows up in the New Testament in other places (Acts 19:29; 20:4; 27:2; Colossians 4:10), and Luke is also a gospel writer and companion of Paul (Colossians 4:14; 2 Timothy 4:11). These are Paul and Timothy's "fellow workers," one of Paul's highest labels for those in his inner circle. These are his trusted gospel companions.

Trusted companions for Paul did not mean they saw eye to eye on everything. Paul was too fiery for that. But through it all they remained close. Eugene Peterson said it so well I close with his words:

> To be a friend to someone does not mean you pamper or indulge him or her. Friendship also involves struggle and loss, tension and turbulence. One of my favorite proverbs is "Faithful are the wounds of a friend" (Proverbs 27:6). A friend, if honest and true, will tell you things you don't want to hear. A friend, if deeply serious about you, will do things that feel painful. Friends do that because they respect our dignity and honor our uniqueness. (*As Kingfishers Catch Fire*, 17)

And, he said later in that sermon, friends are present to one another:

> They visit simply for the pleasure of the other's company. Things don't have to get done in a friendship. Friendship is not a way of accomplishing something but a way of being with another in which we become more authentically ourselves. (*As Kingfishers Catch Fire*, 20)

QUESTIONS FOR REFLECTION AND APPLICATION

1. How do you read Paul's instructions about preparing a guest room? What do you think he meant by including that?

2. What might have been Philemon's objections to Paul's appeal, or the objections of others in the household?

3. How do you think Philemon responded to Paul's appeal?

4. What do the closings and openings of Paul's letters tell us about his wide network of co-laborers?

5. What are your key takeaways from studying the letter to Philemon?

FOR FURTHER READING

Peterson, Eugene. *As Kingfishers Catch Fire: A Conversation on the Ways of God formed by the Words of God*. Colorado Springs: WaterBrook, 2017.